GREAT
WITH
CHILD

ALSO BY BETH ANN FENNELLY

Open House

Tender Hooks

GREAT WITH CHILD

Letters to a
Young Mother

Beth Ann Fennelly

W. W. Norton & Company   New York London

For information about permission to reproduce selections from this book,
write to Permissions, W. W. Norton & Company, Inc., 500 Fifth Avenue,
New York, NY 10110

Manufacturing by The Maple-Vail Book Manufacturing Group
Book design by Anna Oler ⁓

Library of Congress Cataloging-in-Publication Data

Fennelly, Beth Ann, date.
Great with child : letters to a young mother / Beth Ann Fennelly.— 1st ed.
p. cm.
ISBN-13: 978-0-393-06182-5 (hardcover)
ISBN-10: 0-393-06182-5 (hardcover)
1. Fennelly, Beth Ann, date.—Correspondence. 2. Motherhood—
Miscellanea. 3. Mothers—Correspondence. 4. Pregnancy—Miscellanea.
5. Letters. I. Title.
HQ759.F39 2006
306.874'3—dc22

2005025930

W. W. Norton & Company, Inc.,
500 Fifth Avenue, New York, N.Y. 10110
www.wwnorton.com

W. W. Norton & Company Ltd.,
Castle House, 75/76 Wells Street, London W1T 3QT

1 2 3 4 5 6 7 8 9 0

For Claire
and Thomas,
who delivered me

and for their father

CONTENTS

A FEW WORDS ABOUT
THESE LETTERS

When I was a girl, I used to love to play school. Now I'm a college professor and play school for a living; some days I enjoy it
so much that getting a paycheck feels criminal. I teach poetry
writing, so I get to know my students well, often because the students are writing about their lives, and also because those drawn
to poetry tend to be (at least to me) the most interesting. Such
was the case during my second year at Knox College in
Galesburg, Illinois, when a student named Kathleen wrote several moving poems about her mother, dying of cancer. Kathleen
ended up leaving mid-semester to return to Georgia to care for
her mother. I was pregnant, and when I gave birth during finals
week, Kathleen sent a quilt that she and her mother had pieced
during the long evenings in the hospital.

Over the next two years Kathleen and I stayed in touch. I e-mailed her about moving to Oxford, Mississippi, with my husband and our newborn daughter, and teaching at the University of Mississippi. Her e-mails told of her mother's death and then, later, meeting a handsome graduate student, Robert. They fell in love, as people do in this good world, and got married. Robert, studying marine biology, was awarded a postdoctoral fellowship in Alaska. She and Robert visited us before they moved, and it was at our house that Kathleen realized she was pregnant. She panicked—with both parents dead and her friends in Georgia soon to be far away, who would help her, who would coach her through? Well, it turned out, I would. In part to stop her from leaking mascara onto my shoulder, I pledged to write her daily. I fell far short of that goal, but I did enjoy exchanging letters, both because doing so bolstered our friendship, weaving us into that grand circle of women giving and getting advice about children, and also because it let me shape my own reflections about pregnancy and child rearing.

A few months after Kathleen gave birth, her friend Carole got pregnant, and Kathleen asked if Carole could read my letters. A few months later Carole asked if she could share them with a new pregnant friend. In the hope that these letters might be of interest to others, I've allowed them to be reprinted here.

—BAF

GREAT
WITH
CHILD

THE LETTERS
TO KATHLEEN

March 10, 2004
Dear One—
and dear One-within-One:

I rarely write real, old-fashioned letters anymore; hardly anyone does. If he were alive today, Vincent van Gogh wouldn't be writing his passionate letters to his brother Theo explaining that he wanted "to paint men and women with that something of the eternal which the halo used to symbolize." Instead, he'd e-mail, in lowercase, with typos. Though I can't believe he'd "wink" with an asterisk and parenthesis. Let's spare him that imagined indignity.

See, Kathleen, the weight of a pen and thick paper under my hand leads me to a slower pace, slower thoughts, to handpicked words. So let's not despair at waiting out your waiting in without a computer. And after all, doesn't it seem right to be old-fashioned while the baby grows? To garden from seeds and bake bread from yeast . . . really we should be using the ink of cuttlefish and paper boiled in copper pots.

As if in preparation to write you, I've been reading the most marvelous book. It's called *The Pillow Book of Sei Shōnagon*. The name comes from a habit of court women of the Heian culture in the eleventh century, which was to wear hairstyles so elaborate they took hours to arrange. At night, the women slept propped on lacquer pillow boxes to preserve their hairstyles. The box had a drawer where one kept a sort of diary, a "pillow book." Sei Shōnagon, a lady-in-waiting to the Japanese empress, kept a delightful pillow book, full of memoirs, lists, and poems.

Shōnagon often writes of how the empress and the others at court valued skill at letter writing. And letters were more than just an accumulation of words—the calligraphy, the ink, the paper, the manner of folding or twisting it, and the wrapping of the letter in moss or iris roots or mountain sedge—all these added nuances of meaning. There were specific letters for ritualized occasions—for example, after a court woman let a lover spend the night in her room, he'd write her a love letter upon returning home. One lady-in-waiting received her morning letter scented with incense and "attached to a spray of bush-clover, still damp with dew." What a night that man must have had, to need to write her before the sun had dried the grasses!

Well, sweet friend, I have no lotus petals to write on, no iris roots to bind these papers, and my only messenger is the U.S. Postal Service. Furthermore, you've no doubt noticed my handwriting is poor (isn't it curious, K—we've been friends for four years but I think you've never seen my handwriting?), but in a nod to Shōnagon, I choose this pale green paper and my best green Bic pen to write to you, as you are swelling with spring. And so unaccustomed I am to longhand that my fingers are tired already. A thousand miles and several days away as you read this, think of me here in my little Mississippi kitchen, putting down my pen, flexing my hands. And then walking to my desk to choose a stamp—as you've no doubt noticed, Mary Cassatt's *Mother and Child*.

Love and Kisses,
Beth Ann

March 11, 2004
Dear One—

Instead of using our standard calendar, don't you think we should create a new one? I should head this letter: the tenth day of your third month in the year of your baby, who today has formed leg and arms nubbins, who begins to grow fingers and eyelids. Why shouldn't a new era be christened, as it is when a new emperor in Japan ascends the throne? For each birth begins a new dynasty, each birth is mythic, even if it's just to the one being born.

I always envied the story of my sister's birth, so much more dramatic than my own. I'd steal the story if doing so wouldn't make me thirty-four instead of thirty-two. My sister came into the world on July 20, 1969, during the moon launch. My mom tells of laboring in the New Jersey hospital so long that the nurses and doctor had gone down the hall to watch TV—this was a time when women were tied to the cots and anesthetized chin-down, their flesh as heavy and foreign as the lead shield a dentist lays on a patient's chest before an X-ray. Finally Mom was aware that the baby was crowning, more than crowning, and she called to the nurses, who ran down the hallway on their spongy white shoes and guided my furious yellow-tinged sister into the world in a rush of blood-streaked headwaters just as Neil Armstrong took that first fateful step, the Sea of Tranquility his backdrop, and she could hear down the hall the out-of-this-world TV voice—*One small step for man . . .*

And was my mother any less of a hero than he? Is any mother?

Love,
Beth Ann

March 13, 2004
Dear One,

This afternoon I went to a Quaker wedding—I'd never been to one before. The bride and groom walk in separately, state their vows, then sit together as "the meeting continues in silent waiting upon God while those assembled share in the worship through prayer and meditation"—this according to the pamphlet handed out. I'm so used to ceremonies loud with music and proclamations that at first the suspended hush made me nervous. But then I began to relax into the silence, to let what could happen happen.

I started thinking how getting married and having (or at least making) a baby are events taken on by two individuals, but they gain additional meaning through being celebrated in society. I've become a believer in the power of rituals—something I scoffed at as a teenager when I was a good member of my tribe, ironic and antiromantic with my R.E.M. T-shirts and wristfuls of black rubber bracelets. Matrimony held no appeal—why not just live together unshackled? And at twenty-four, when I met Tommy on the first day of our grad program in writing at the University of Arkansas, we did exactly that. We moved in together in a little box of a house and made eight hundred dollars a month teaching freshmen where to stick their commas, while Tommy stuck me just as often as we could. We were so poor that after teaching class I'd cross the hall to the restroom and load my backpack with pilfered toilet paper. At the grocery store, I'd triple-bag each potato so I wouldn't have to buy Ziplocs for my lunches. A poster in the kitchen covered the hole where a drunken friend head-butted the wall at a party.

About two years into our relationship, Tommy and I made one of the biggest commitments two writers can make. We were sitting on the floor in front of the couch, figuring how to make the rent. It had been another night of lentils and rice. All around us were bookcases—our separate bookcases. We hadn't merged our books, on the silent assumption that when we split up we'd both want our books back. But gradually we were realizing that there would be no splitting up in our future. I don't remember who first suggested it—maybe we thought of it simultaneously—but suddenly we sprang at the bookshelves, making giddy piles of duplicates. Then we loaded up Tommy's Nissan and headed to the used book store, which we left sometime later with a fat check. After paying rent, we even had a little money left to dine at Belvedere's. I still remember my meal, chicken breast topped with artichokes, bacon, and sun-dried tomatoes in a light goat cheese sauce. That night, holding hands across the white tablecloth, I think we both knew our futures were linked. We who hoped to make our livings with words weren't ready to use them yet to describe what was happening, but I gazed at Tommy's face across the table, he was gazing back at me, and we held our eyes so long that the Christmas lights behind him grew blurry and haloed. I felt dizzy realizing that I was gazing at the face of the man I would marry. So, in many ways, selling those books felt more momentous than accepting an engagement ring from Tommy the following Christmas.

We looked to the wedding as a big party, but I didn't imagine we'd emerge from it *changed*. After all, how much more married could we get? Nevertheless, marriage deepened our relationship. Part of this deepening came from inside, as we relaxed into the idea of forever, put our weight down in our shared hopes. But another part of it came from undergoing this ritual sanctioned by society. Making our vows public allowed us to dream about ourselves in the presence of others and to feel their support. Some friends offered testimonials to marriage's quiet joys, which, because they aren't dramatic, often don't get told. All of this impressed on us the profundity of our decision in a way we couldn't have felt if we were merely "shacking up."

And it was hard to keep an ironic distance from social convention when gifts began to overflow my mom's dining room and spread onto her kitchen table. Sometimes on the gift cards people wrote surprisingly emotional notes about how much we meant to them—and this was another way matrimony taught me how deep our communal bonds go. Sometimes the cards and gifts were from folks we hardly knew, usually my mom's friends. I'd be opening some beautiful box and find, perhaps, a place setting (how I love my china, the plate brims striped with mint green, bordered with gold, so pretty they make food taste better), and I'd think each time, But they hardly *know* me! Gradually I realized that this outpouring wasn't about me. It wasn't personal. It was better than personal.

And now I love giving nice wedding gifts to younger couples, taking my place in the cycle. Which is just an outward sign, I suppose, of how being married made me become more fully part of the world.

But Kathleen, being a mother does it more, a thousand times more. First, you understand yourself as lodged in history in a way you didn't before. Your beliefs will be tested, your hypotheses put into action, so you'll consider them in a new way. Whether you're explaining where pets go when they die or teaching your child to recycle, your philosophies have ramifications. For the rest of history, echoes of your voice will be heard.

Also, you will be knitted more tightly into the social fabric because you'll need help. You'll feel vulnerable—as if you're condemned to wear that hospital gown that opens in the back. But you'll also feel bolstered because so many people you ask for help (and many you don't) will give it. You'll exchange independence for the benefits of community, the needing and being needed. For you will be needed as well; a new mother and child are a powerful renewing force. When you push your stroller past a group of elderly women, you'll see in the turning gladness of their bodies a glimpse of the children they had been turning toward the tin music of the ice cream van. On September 11, 2001, Claire was a few months old, and we'd just moved to Oxford. In the days that followed the attacks, many neighbors and new friends stopped by to make sure we were okay. Inside, they gravitated to Claire's bassinet, wanting to smell her, to hold her, to watch her guileless slate-blue eyes open. I understood these guests not only wanted to see if we needed anything but also needed her.

Do you remember in *How the Grinch Stole Christmas!* when the Grinch is alone on the mountain after plundering the Christmas of the Whos down below, and his heart swells to three times its normal size? That's the other thing that happens when you become a mom. You feel more deeply. You become capable of a raw, scary fullness of emotion that tenderizes the hardened muscle of the heart. And it endangers you. Because you feel for other people's suffering more than you used to, especially for the suffering of children, as if the love you bear for your child is so outsized that it can't be contained but splashes out into the world, your salty tears brimming the salty oceans. The babies abandoned in dumpsters, or starving in war-blasted countries—your swollen heart is their fertile target.

Motherhood makes you stronger even as it makes you weaker. Your new sensitivity is a strength, and you should see it that way. Because others might see it as something to deride. If a Sally Struthers charity plea makes you cry in front of the TV, tears splatting the head of your nursing baby, don't let others dismiss you as hormonal, though hormones may be a factor. Don't make light of the emotional expansion of motherhood as something aberrant, something that needs to be medicated away.

Time for me to close, dear K. I bought a whole chicken at the farmers' market, and some soft rosemary goat cheese. I think I can approximate Chicken Belvedere if I'm clever. Think how good the house will smell when Claire Bear wakes from her nap and yells with lusty lungs, MOOOOOMMMMYYYYYYYYYYY—

Love you,
Beth Ann

March 15, 2004
Dear K,

As you were here for the saga, I thought you'd like an update—after exhausting north Mississippi's entire M&M supply, Claire is officially potty-trained. She's had three whole days in big-girl panties. I may even let her go back to drinking liquids again. Ha.

Oh the joy in passing up the Pampers aisle in the grocery store! I feel like I've added a hundred bucks to my take-home pay.

Hey, have you ever noticed that our culture pays lip service to the idea of men doing half of the child rearing, yet the baby supplies are stocked right next to the tampons? Why not pop some diapers over by the jock itch spray, the rack of *Field & Stream?* Miss you—

Beth Ann

March 18, 2004
Dear K—

The erotics of motherhood—in our culture it's taboo. Well, I suppose it *is* terrifying. That hunger for the tiny naked body and the need to hold it against one's own naked body. The intoxicant of baby's head, baby's mouth (without teeth, they can't have bad breath—it's teeth that harbor the germs). The hair-thin veins in their sleeping, twitching eyelids; their malleable, see-through ears; the teardrop glottis at the back of their throats vibrating with anger and hunger while you're fumbling with the buttons of your blouse, then your nursing bra, and your breasts feel the surge of warm milk rushing to the ducts, and finally the child has at it, the braided sweet river is sluicing down her tongue, she is drifting in the boat of your arms with her tiny fingers over the side, rippling the water, easy as Sunday morning. It's all so damn *physical.*

I remember gazing at Claire and realizing I didn't just love her, I was *in love* with her. She was the most stimulating company I could imagine. Realizing also that Tommy was at a bit of a distance from us—not that we chose that, but with Claire and me, rocking in the chair, grazing and gazing and humming—we were just so sufficient. She'd suck herself to sleep, blissed out in my arms, then fall off the nipple with her lips open and her tongue still flexing a time or two, her body completely relaxed, drunk as a hobo on my lovejuice. Tommy would want to help. Did I want him to pick Claire up and transfer her to her bassinet so I could get some work done? No, I did not. I wanted to watch her as she slept. Wasn't there anything, anything I wanted? I'd think for a moment—then I'd decide on a glass of water, so he had something to give.

The expression *I could eat you up* is no hyperbole. Once when Claire was about one and a half, and in this phase when she always wanted to "sand up in the cabiner"—stand up on the counter and paw through the jars of baby food—I was behind her, steadying her, and her chubby round bottom was right in front of my face and I couldn't help myself, I leaned forward and gave her right peachy-cheek a little love bite. Um, harder than I meant to. She turned around with a shocked look, and, more from surprise than pain, I hope, let out a cry; then fat tears were rolling down her fat cheeks. I, too, was shocked.

Before I had Claire I'd try to understand what the love for a child could be like, so I thought about other kinds of love—love for

Tommy, for my mother, for my college roommates. Although motherlove ends up being a wholly new experience, it indeed has elements of those other loves. Including erotic love—though that challenges our idealized notion of motherhood. Those first few times I had to leave Claire for a few hours—no matter how much I thought I needed a break before the break occurred—well, the yearning to return to her was not unlike the yearning I'd feel for Tommy those heady days in Arkansas when we'd make love several times a night, then I'd be off to teach my freshman comp class smelling of sex and cherry-blow pops, my lips swollen from kissing. Standing at the chalkboard, I'd feel a rush of vertigo at the thought of him waiting back at his place in his Scooby-Doo boxers.

I remember my first overnight trip away from Claire to give a poetry reading—I was sick with missing her, and when I called home I wanted to know the most mundane details of her eating and sleeping and even her bowel movements. After a pause, I asked, "What is she wearing?" and we both laughed.

Well, Kathleen, I'll be interested to hear what you have to say about this in about, hmmm, six months.

Love,
Beth Ann

March 19, 2004
Dear One,

Yesterday, I came across a *New York Times Magazine* from September 7, 2003, with an article called "The Futile Pursuit of Happiness." It discussed the findings of researchers in "affective forecasting"—sociologists who study happiness by asking people to forecast what they believe will make them happy in the future, then later, after the event has happened, comparing their predictions with their reported happiness. And what these researchers have found is that we're poor predictors of what future events will bring us joy. The researchers gave several examples, including this—that despite people's predictions to the contrary, "Having children does nothing to improve well-being, even as it drives marital satisfaction dramatically down."

It's an alarming statement. Part of me wants to assure you that raising a child improves well-being and leads to a stronger marriage. Which can happen, of course—I'd like to think it happened for me. But it's also true that many marriages are on shaky ground after the baby is brought home—in fact, it's one of the most common times for divorce.

Some of the new stresses on the marriage are obvious. It would be difficult to overstate how crazy and stupid lack of sleep can make a person—now get two such folks together and throw in a baby, especially if it's a screamer, and you'll find why sleep deprivation is a successful technique in cult indoctrination. Oh, yes the couple is now indoctrinated in a cult, the Cult of Baby, and their sleep is "a dirty torn cloth," as the poet Alicia Ostriker writes. Then there are the money worries. And it's a true challenge for the new parents to find time to relax, go to the movies, play sports. For the mother, there are the physical changes, her depression about the extra pounds, the loose muscles that trickle out a drop of pee when she sneezes. Add to that her compromised wardrobe, the epaulettes of spit-up. Now her hair (what's left of it after the hormone-shedding "fourth trimester") is always in a ponytail to save it from the yank of baby fists, the same fists which keep her ears free of hoop earrings. And every day is a "fat jeans" day. No wonder she has a lower sex drive, which frustrates the husband, who is already dealing with the fact that if his wife is breast-feeding, his former beauty queen is now a Dairy Queen.

These rather superficial changes might be discussed in the parenting handbooks, but there are stresses beyond these that aren't mentioned so often. I'm thinking about how my generation is the first to expect men and women to be equal breadwinners, but when baby comes, this perception often changes. We can't look to our parents to see how to negotiate work/family switches, because our mothers had a different attitude toward work. Many knew all along that they'd stop working when they started a family, and didn't define themselves according to their jobs. Quitting was easier and didn't necessarily require significant shifts in income or self-esteem.

Not so anymore. Now, if a couple wants and is able to put off full-time day care for the new baby, they have few options.

Because it rarely works out that both parents can cut back and keep their jobs, the couple must choose one spouse to cut back or stop working entirely, and it's usually the woman. Often she feels lucky about this, feels blessed to be able to nourish the baby those first weeks, months, or even years. I know I did—and when I think about my desire to have another child, I hope to spend the first year at home again. Fortunately, in the academic world, it's relatively easy to take an unpaid leave—*if* the family can afford it. For other careers, the woman might never regain her status after returning to work.

And so, even if the woman relishes staying home with the baby, little eddies of discontent begin to swirl in the formerly calm waters of the marriage. She feels she's stagnating. Soon her résumé is as outdated as the suits hanging in the back of her closet. Since we live in a society that values success in dollar terms, her contributions to the family economy approach invisibility—after all, she "doesn't work." Some of my friends no longer feel they can spend money on themselves the way their husbands do. Or they resent asking their husbands for money. And the husband resents being resented—while she complains of boredom, he envies her at home in her slippers, singing along to Barney, straining homemade baby food.

These marriage stresses could be lessened by a government that offered paid parental leave for both spouses and encouraged the creation of flexible working arrangements. But for all the current administration's talk of "family values," these goals seem a long way off. Until then, modern families need to understand how rough this transition can be, and be patient with their spouses, and themselves, and look to the experience of families who've managed well, and continue to pressure policy makers to offer working solutions for working families.

Maybe you and Robert will sail through these waters without any treacherous shoals; maybe thinking about them in advance will help. I hope so. And maybe by the time our children have children, they will see the ways we struggled and be wiser. That would be a good thing to give them.

Love,
Beth Ann

March 21, 2004
Dear K,

Just got back from the park with Claire where we saw darling six-month-old twin boys, fat as Buddhas in little sailor suits. Their little forearms were so soft and fat, their little hands so soft and fat, their wrists merely creases in the fat, as if rubber bands were cinched there. Their legs looked screwed on. It put me in mind of that line from the Lyle Lovett song, "Fat babies have no pride."

I love best the creases in a fat baby's thighs. The Italians have a word for those rolls—*goshi*. I hear there's a Yiddish word, too. Hmm, I'll have to ask Gavin if there's a Gaelic one. Probably there isn't—Irish history isn't studded with fat babies. Quite the contrary. My ancestors came to this country because their babies were starving. You know about the potato famine in the 1840s, of course—but did you know that there was enough food, that no one needed to die, much less over a million people? Even when the potatoes blackened with rot, the fields were tasseled with wheat. But the rich English landlords demanded the wheat as rent payment. If the Irish didn't pay up, they were imprisoned or killed; if they did, they died from hunger.

And so the Fennellys and the Sullivans and the Nolans and the McNamaras boarded the coffin ships for America, and those who lived planted what they had, and what they planted here grew, including those who grew those who grew me. And now there's little left in Ireland that shows my people ever lived and died there, just a few names in the records of a country church or two, some gravestones hushed by fingers of moss . . . but I hear there still stands a pub in Kilkenny called "Fennelly's," and I'll take Claire there one day for a pint of Guinness ("It's good for you"), and some beef stew, with potatoes.

On the topic of fat babies, do you know Brady Udall's book *The Miracle Life of Edgar Mint?* If not, let me send you a copy, it's

fabulous. Anyway, he stayed with us one time when he was giving a reading at Square Books, bringing along his wife, their two
sons, and their baby girl Georgia, maybe the fattest, cutest little
baby I've ever seen. Anyway, this baby was so fat that her chins
tripled and quadrupled on her fat little neck. And because babies
dribble milk down their chins, and her chin folds were so deep,
she got—are you ready for this—a yeast infection. *Between her
chins.* They had to rub Georgia's chins with Vagisil to clear it up.
Brady said when he'd pick her up from her crib in the morning,
she'd smell like a loaf of bread.

Love,
Beth Ann

March 22, 2004
Dear Kathleen—

I too had strange, off-kilter pregnant dreams, dreams in which
my breasts swelled like balloons, dreams in which I rolled over in
bed and nearly suffocated a mysteriously shrunken Tommy,
dreams in which I towered over knee-high students, or I kept
shape-shifting, like Lewis Carroll's Alice.

It's pretty alarming to feel invaded by a body snatcher. As much as I loved feeling Claire move inside me, it could also be distracting. I'd be reading a book when she'd start her gymnastic routine, and I'd end up reading her instead, trying to guess which body part was causing my stomach's contortions. Was that her heel against the bowl of my belly like a spatula scraping peanut butter from the jar? And then I'd see that ten minutes had passed and I hadn't read a word, so focused was I on my portable entertainment center . . .

We accept that we live in a world of chaos theory. We're constantly reminded of the basic instability of "facts." For example, an article I read in *The Atlantic* explains that scientists who've gotten a closer look at Pluto no longer think it's a planet and might demote it to a "small body." So even our basic schoolhouse truths, like the numbers of planets in our solar system, can be rehauled, revised. In the face of such uncertainty, we turn for comfort to the things we know, such as our physical nature, the kinesthetic feeling of our dependable bodies walking this earth. But then pregnancy comes and our bodies morph, something inside moves without our volition, our centers of gravity tilt and whirl, our identities tilt and whirl, men look and talk to us differently, our appetites and habits change, and we barely recognize ourselves.

One night toward the end of my pregnancy, when I could only sleep fitfully and on my side with a pillow between my knees and another under my hip (we called them "Tommy blockers"), I dreamt that I was a young bride again, wearing my wedding dress, alone in the house, cleaning the floors. I heard a cheery whistle and looked down the hallway through the front door where a handsome dark-haired man was strolling by, tossing his keys in the air and catching them. He turned his head, sighted me, and halted. Then he dropped his keys, nearly falling over himself to scramble up the path to my front door. I demurely ducked into a side room, but he waited, hoping to get a glimpse of me in my billowy gown—you see, he'd fallen in love with me and was absolutely powerless to leave. He was calling, "I have to see you! Please, tell me your name!" when, like a predictable sitcom, the alarm went off, tearing me from the pleasant fog of his desire. It was terrible to slowly push myself to sitting and look down at my impossible stomach, my huge thighs splayed beneath it all bacon-fatty with my varicose (very gross) veins, and think that no sane man would ever desire me again. To top it all off, I felt chagrined—dreaming of myself in my wedding dress, how unoriginal. I felt like a John Cheever character.

There: I've shared this vain recollection so you feel better. Good thing I'm not your teacher anymore, you'd have no respect for me.

Listen, sugar, about your baby-weight worries—if you want to lose the weight, you will. But you won't lose it like the Hollywood stars who lose forty-five pounds in two months by exercising for three hours a day. We mortals don't have the three hours or the personal trainer—or the airbrushed photos. They say you should give yourself as long to take off the weight as you did to put it on, and for once, they've said something worthwhile.

What I did was join a gym that provided day care. That first year I was home with Claire, and at first it seemed like paradise, and then I began to get a little—dare I admit it—bored. So afternoons, I'd stroll Claire over to Orion Fitness, leave her in the capable hands of Miss Leigh or Miss Carol, and do my little gerbil routine, a quick round on the weight machines and stairclimber. It worked, eventually.

But you know what? I still can't wear my wedding dress. It fits in the waist, and in the bust (my bust is actually smaller than before due to the breast-feeding). The dress doesn't fit because it can't close over my back—my rib cage expanded as my lungs shifted to make room for the baby. Somehow the rib cage not fitting seems fitting. Claire expanded my world from the inside out. Why shouldn't the twin streams of my breathing shift in their riverbeds? Why shouldn't my ribs cage the memory of holding my breath over that cathedral I filled with the other?

Love,
Beth Ann

March 27, 2004
Dear One,

You're almost done with your first trimester—congrats, buttercup. Soon you should be feeling better, and soon you'll be able to tell people that you're expecting. Now your baby is three inches long, the length of your finger. By next month, your baby will be the size of an apple, and you'll probably start showing, too. And then you'll be in that awkward stage where your regular jeans are too tight but wearing maternity jeans feels like wearing a deflated hot-air balloon. Here's a tip: you can wear your regular jeans for another month with the rubber-band trick. Thread the rubber band through your buttonhole and loop the ends around your button. Wear long shirts and no one will catch on.

By the end of month four, I was visibly pregnant and glad to be past those weeks when I merely looked like I'd eaten a big lunch. Months five, six, and seven for me were a dream—I felt like an earth goddess, and my hair grew long and glossy, and my nails were nearly impossible to break. Months eight and nine were harder—I've always been a back sleeper, and suddenly there were only two options, the right side and the left side. Getting from one to the other required a six-point turn. And I was peeing hourly because someone had parked a Mack truck on my bladder. It got to the point where I felt if I wanted a glass of water, I should drink it in the bathroom. Also, I got cranky with being a Public Figure, strangers observing, "You look ready to pop," as I walked by. I wanted to walk into a bar and order up a round of tequila, just to watch everyone freak. Not that anyone would serve a woman so pregnant that her sneakers were tied off-center because she could no longer bend over enough to tie them in the middle.

There were days when I wished I were a sea horse, because it's the male of the species that gives birth. The female sea horse ejects her eggs—about six hundred total—into the male, and he releases sperm over them. He harbors the fertilized eggs for about fifty days, and then he births them one by one in violent contortions. He has to be careful to empty his pouch completely, or the rotting corpse of an offspring might cause him to die.

If humans could choose either the man or woman to give birth, I wonder how many couples would choose the man? Somehow, I think not many. Women are so much tougher—I'd always guessed that but knew for certain after my hours in the spotlit delivery room, and after talking to girlfriends about their deliveries. I remember as a girl reading a biography of Harriet B. Tubman, the escaped slave who brought hundreds of other African-Americans to freedom though the Underground Railroad. A few years before she escaped from her plantation, she went into labor while picking cotton. She lay down in the furrow, delivered her child, cut the umbilical cord and knotted it, put her baby in a sling across her chest, and kept picking.

Love,
Beth Ann

March 29, 2004
Dear K,

I'm writing you in a disco. Okay, it's not a disco, it just feels like one, because Claire has discovered that if she climbs on top of my file cabinet, she can reach my light switch. On, off, on, off, it's like living under a strobe light. And now that I think about it, living under a strobe light is a pretty good metaphor for life with a toddler. Although I play with her, dress her, feed her, bathe her little body every day (well, almost every day), each time I look, she seems in a different place, almost a different person, without any kind of transition, like a dancer under a strobe light.

At night before turning in, either Tommy or I check on our sleeping child. When we do, sometimes what we find is not the infant that we rocked to sleep but a large, gangly, grown-up girl. Gone are the days when we'd have to scan the crib until we found her, no bigger than a pair of rolled-up socks in the laundry basket. Instead, she's stretched from end to end of the suddenly cramped crib. I call my husband. "Look," I whisper. "She's huge!" He shakes his disbelieving head. We've been similarly stunned to see her in the tub and find that sleek seal body has replaced the fat-creased infant we expected, reminding us of those "magic cap-sule" sponges that swells one hundred times its original size.

And it's not only physically that she seems to leap without transition—it's emotionally and cognitively, too. First, she's Mommy's baby, and when she wakes up, only Mommy can get her milk, only Mommy can change her diaper. But then without reason or warning, she's Daddy's girl. She will brush her teeth only if Daddy holds the brush. She will eat only if Daddy makes the pasta. Mommy feels left out and rejected. *But Daddy's a bad cook!* Mommy wants to shout. No use. If Mommy wants to help, she can clean around the high chair, from which Claire flings coins of hot dogs like the queen of Mardi Gras.

Then the week comes when Claire regresses, stops potty-training or feeding herself and refuses her formerly beloved task of pressing down the Velcro on her sneakers. The next week, how-ever, she screams if we don't let her dress herself, and I wheel her through Kroger in her nightie, winter boots, swim floaties, and cowboy hat. Even with Claire's imagination, we can't keep up. She tells me, "I the baby, you the mommy." Okay, I think I can handle that. Then she decides *she's* the mommy. I cram my thumb in my mouth obligingly. Then Daddy wants to play. "Who's Daddy?" I ask Claire. "Scooby-Doo," she says. "Am I Shaggy?" I ask. "Cinderella, pay attention," she warns, "or you'll get a time-out."

Why, I wonder, are toddlers like this? It's enough to drive me crazy. More than once it has. Like this morning, when I've run too many errands before taking Claire to the park. We're both tired when we get there. I hand her a few Gummi Bears, but she flings them to the ground. "Orange and yellow! Bad bears!" I'd forgotten, Claire was only eating green food today. I fish a few green ones out. "No! Now the green ones are dirty!" I blow on the green bears, rub them on my skirt, but by now she's so worked up that when she reaches for them she knocks them into the playground mulch. And begins howling. I'm tired, I'm annoyed, I'm mashing a Gummi Bear against my daughter's clamped teeth, yelling, "Eat it! Eat it, you brat!" And then I stop, look up into the blue, restrained sky, and laugh a little. I hug Claire, who, after all, is simply trying to impose rules on a world of flux so she can have a sense of control.

There's a Chinese curse that says, "May you live in interesting times." With toddlers around, times are always interesting. As adults, we change so grudgingly that daylight saving throws us off for a week. But in Claire's world, she can reach the faucet today when only yesterday she couldn't. And she learns a new word at a minimum of every two hours, according to language theorists. Her progress is not all linear, though, because suddenly she can't remember what the animal doctor is called and her fingers can't pinch the marble from the cup and pee-pee is running from her big-girl panties into her Dora sneakers. It must be terrifying to be so interesting.

One of the hardest things about parenting toddlers is that we have to live in flux again. On good days, I adopt an almost Zen-like stance, and content myself with immersion into the Now. On bad days, I feel almost betrayed, panicky that I can't stop her passing from phase to phase even long enough to fully appreciate each one. But of course if we could stop the journey, it wouldn't be so compelling, so consuming.

Now Claire pauses at the platform at the top of the jungle gym—she hasn't gone down the big-kid slide before. She looks at it, holding her breath, and I expect her to grasp the rails and back down. I find that I, too, am holding my breath, *hoping* that she'll grasp the rails and back down. But this is the whimful toddler world, and I'm along for the ride. "Mommy," she calls, "I'm a big girl now." And with terrible speed, she hurls her precious body down the slide.

Love,
Beth Ann

April 1, 2004
Dear One,

I can scarcely believe you need my advice when I think of how confident you are. I remember your visit, how you woke up early and came into the kitchen in your Hello Kitty pj's and took a sip from the coffee mug I handed you, then turned and poured the rest down the drain. "Strange," you said, rinsing the mug, "I used to love coffee, and now it makes me feel kind of sick." You looked up then, and slowly turned to me as I raised my eyes to meet yours: a pregnant pause. I went to fetch a test (I buy them in bulk) while you went to wake Robert. Sweet Robert—with that linebacker's body and deep voice, no one would guess him so sentimental. Remember how he said, "We'll keep this pregnancy test forever"? You answered, "Great, a family heirloom. 'Look, kids, a stick I peed on.'"

Yet I also remember how scared you were by lunchtime, after things had sunk in a bit. You were cross-legged on the couch, rocking, hugging a pillow, as if foreshadowing the belly you'd grow, repeating, "We're not ready. We're not ready."

So I continue to offer what I can. What I want to say today, sweet friend, is no matter how busy you become as the mother of a newborn, make sure you read in a good book every day, even if it's just for a few minutes. Of course there will be Required Reading, the baby books and magazines, and they'll help you with your questions and keep you from wondering whether you're going crazy. But find time to read good literature, too, even if a novel takes a month.

You'll hear people say how absorbing babies are. Which sounds like we're water and they're sponges. In a way, that's not far from the truth. There's an emptying of the self that's very freeing, very pleasurable. Whole hours could go by when I did nothing, desired nothing more than to gaze at Claire's sleeping face (and occasionally hold my finger beneath her nose to make sure she was breathing). This is the "hood" of motherhood, as we are like horses with blinders on, but what we are looking at is so beautiful we have no desire for greener pastures, at last. For the first time in my life I felt empty of ambition. None of my usual self-criticism, no anxiety about falling behind. None of my "Why haven't I heard back from *The Paris Review?*" or "What writing sample should I send for the Lowell Scholarship?" Sometimes, watching Claire, I seemed to enter a trance that felt—well, spiritual. As Simone Weil writes, "Absolute attention is prayer."

But it's also true that a new mother can feel like she's trapped in a pointillist painting, too overwhelmed by details to make out a pattern. The eight-pound baby makes many pounds of laundry, laundry that must be washed separately. Each pacifier that tumbles from her pucker must be sterilized. A new landscape of lotions and potions colonizes the new changing table—rash, thrush, cradle cap, and gas, each needs its own expensive remedy. The part of your brain formerly reserved for Deep Thoughts now seems hogged by choking hazards, developmental milestones, broken-English instructions for baby gadgets that are never quite ready-to-assemble. So it's easy to believe you don't have time for luxuries like showering, not to mention reading.

But remember that reading provides nourishment for hungers we might not even be aware of. How often have I chosen a book at random and found in it an answer I didn't realize I was seeking.

As if great books are vitamins that sense our deficiencies. Reading educates the emotions, and reading informs our decision making, for we learn through the experiences of others as well as our own.

So reading is one of those things that seems selfish but, in the end, makes us better mothers. And by reading, we're raising children who'll love reading. I learned this from a study that found two things in common among children who grow up to be readers. I might have guessed, before reading the article, that these things were parents who stress reading and who read bedtime stories to their kids. While both of these things surely help, it turns out that the two crucial criteria for future readers are that they live in "print-rich environments" (houses with lots of books) and that they see their caregivers read daily. So keep reading, dear K, as happily this is one of those times when what's good for you is good for your child.

Love,
Beth Ann

April 6, 2004
Dear One,

The wife of one of my colleagues in the English Department is pregnant and I can't keep my eyes off her. At the department potluck last week, I had to remind myself not to stare. I'd watch her pass a plate to someone, then I'd follow her hands as they unconsciously returned to her belly. I remember toward the end of my pregnancy that the side where Claire's back was curled would be warmer than the other side. Often, I could feel the firm curve of her little butt, the size of a doorknob, just to the right of my belly button, and it filled my palm perfectly. No matter what else I was doing, I'd also be touching her. Whether teaching or walking or eating an apple, some part of me was musing on our mystery, the love that felt ageless and wise. Such a laying on of hands, such a daily walking embrace.

I can't stop watching this pregnant woman because I'm looking to her as a tuning fork, trying to sound out my heart to see how I'd feel if we didn't have another child. The truth is, Tommy and I lately have wondered whether we will. We've been trying for almost nine months now, and it keeps not happening. Partially this is due to our travels—often one of us is out of town during my ovulation. So it's not so much that I think we need to see a fertility expert as I think we need to decide how much we want to make a sibling for Claire.

Every month when I get my period, I have a conflicted mess of emotions, because while it's true that I've always envisioned myself as the mother of more than one child, it's also true that as the months roll on, we've really hit our stride with Claire's routines. I almost wrote "we've gotten our lives back," but that makes it sound like what we've been doing hasn't been living. Not so! But we're less frantically baby-centered. We've added back into our schedules things we had to drop for a while. Even something as simple as writing you several times a week isn't something I could do with a newborn in the house. Recently I read Elizabeth Bishop's collected letters and found that there were days when she wrote forty of them! Bishop had no children. If we have another child, I won't be writing letters or poems or much of anything. I'll have to reintroduce myself to the privation of the mind in favor of the body, at least for most of that first year. I can't manage to forget the devastating equation a female writer once announced to the class I was taking in grad school: each child you have equals two books you won't write. The poet Keith Waldrop put it even more succinctly: "Keep out of reach of children."

When I recall Claire's early months, the terrible mind-numbing fatigue, how very stupid I felt all the time, all poetry and clear thoughts receding like an archipelago of islands on the horizon, I'm not sure how eager I am to go back to that shore. What baby-crazed night was it that I woke to feed Claire and woke again to calm her crying and woke again for the same reason, and at last I sat rocking her, eyes closed, mumbling a few songs, and I realized that the ABC song and "Twinkle, Twinkle, Little

Star" had the same melody? I swear, it seemed like I'd discovered gravity.

A few years later I learned doctors actually have a term for this: placenta brain. Apparently, many new mothers suffer a short-term memory loss for facts that have nothing to do with their infants, while retaining a better-than-usual short-term memory for baby-related data. It's nature's way of ensuring a baby's caregiver is paying attention. How I wish I knew back then that my stupidity was a common reaction; I thought I was losing my mind. How comforting! A name! What I had had a name!

So there are moments in each day when I'm sure: no more children. But. But. But. I'm seized with incredible longings to hold a newborn again. When I think that I would never hold another child to my naked breast—never wake to the child's half cry and lift it to my pillow where it rolls toward me and with a frantic mouth begins unwinding the skein of warm milk, gradually losing the jerky anxiousness, quelling toward calm, the tiny fist-buds unfolding, the eyeballs rolling back in drunken bliss—I feel tremendous sadness. And of course there's Claire's desire, although she's just started to voice it, for a sibling. How lonely family vacations might be without a conspirator to share the backseat, bisected with its imaginary line that neither can cross. I also imagine a future in which Tommy and I are old and sick and the burden of care falls on her. I see her standing alone before a grave, and I want to paint in a brother or sister to put an arm around her.

And when I read these words of Anna Akhmatova, I yearn to say them and have them be true about me as well: "The secret of secrets is inside me again."
Love,
Beth Ann

April 8, 2004
Hello, Sweet Thang—

Truly, babies are hyphenated—they are endearing-exasperating; they are amusing-annoying. But the phases go so quickly that nothing is unbearably bad (or good) for long. That's why every phase is so bittersweet, for even as you are pleased to dress the child in a never-before-worn outfit, you grieve the tiny outfit suddenly too small—how lovely she was in this lavender dress from Monica, I always thought she'd get a few more wears out of it . . . so their infancy passes in a wave of nostalgia that swells and swells but never crests, never recedes.

The phase I was most excited for was when Claire would learn to speak, but even so I mourned in advance the loss of the babble bubble, the noisy silence of not-words, before the world joined in. In exchange for the marvelous poetry of childspeak, we gave up our language of gesture and symbol and significant looks. Preverbal Claire would motion for raisins by turning her hand palm down, bunching her fingers together and bobbing her wrist. It took me a while to realize this gesture imitated my hand picking raisins from the canister. Then came the day when she said "ray-ray," and didn't need the hand motion anymore, which I missed. Now she says "raisins," and I find myself missing "ray-ray." The books I've read say it's best to address children in full sentences and avoid baby talk, but I confess that once or twice, for nostalgia's sake, I've asked, "Claire, do you want some ray-rays?" But she greets the question blankly. "Ray-ray is what you said before you could talk much," I tell her. "Oh, yes," she mock-remembers, "that was when I was zero years old and there was dinosaurs."

But while something irreplaceable is lost when they enter the world of language, what is gained is rewarding indeed. "That hurts some of my feelings." "Daddy, you can't eat wif us, we eat girl cheese sandwiches." "Where are Santa's claws?" "Worm, I make mud for you because I'm your friend." I love to hear her "talk" on the "phone," as she did before I put her down for her nap, placing the remote control against her ear. "Hi, Jess," she said, then concluded with, "Well, I don't want to keep you. I'm very busy today."

There's a book by Steven Pinker called *The Language Instinct* that discusses how language is something we're hardwired for. Language is a fundamental drive, proof of which, according to Pinker, lies in the fact that children acquire language skills they haven't been taught. An example is the recent invention of sign language in Nicaragua. Until 1979, there was no Nicaraguan sign language because deaf people in that country were isolated from each other and so had no opportunity to speak. When the Sandinista government allowed deaf people to form communities, a pidgin language sprang up which allowed for basic communication. The speakers of this sign language were rather like adults who come to learn a second language late in life—their grammar rules were inconsistent and their gestures more like pantomime, full of circumlocutions. However, when young deaf children were introduced into this community, they instinctively created a standardized, expressive grammar. They perfected the language beyond what they needed to communicate with the older generation—that's how strong the language instinct is.

Cognitive psychologists also show that children instinctively create metaphors as soon as they learn language. The ability to use metaphors is so tied to the ability to learn that only when children can make metaphors, some argue, can they make memories. This explains why we don't remember events that happen to us before the age of two or three, according to Douglas R. Hofstadter in "Analogy as the Core of Cognition." He argues that analogies and metaphors are the primary way we experience the world. Because both involve comparisons, we need a certain amount of basic experience—a backlog of life, if you will—in order to have something to compare the something to. Babies lack this raw material, and therefore can't make the comparisons. Only after more life experience is gained can a baby "chunk" events in a way that connects them and makes them memorable. This theory makes me happy—that metaphor, the heart of poetry, is the heart of learning. Girl, I knew it all along.

Watching Claire learn to speak reminds me of my own language study—not so much the Spanish in high school or the French in graduate school as the year after college when I lived in the coal mining village on the Czech-Polish border. When I arrived there, I spoke no Czech, and no one spoke English (under Communism, English had been outlawed). So I threw myself into the language with the desperation of someone who needed to say "potatoes" at the market or would go home without potatoes. This consuming desire to communicate is something I see in toddlers, who act like they've been handed labeling guns to take aim at their world: "ball, ball, doggie, cookie." Their patterns of language immersion seem similar to what mine were—around age two, they use "telegraphic speech," which means they are reduced to essential words. While the word order is correct, grammar isn't. They speak only in the present tense, like I did in the Czech Republic, which somehow gave rise to the impression that there was no past or future, which perhaps explains why I was so wild that year (that, and the Czech beer, and the beautiful sad-eyed men). Two-year-olds ignore verb endings, possessives, and plurals, and all sentences depend strongly on context and interpretation by an adult. I should say a "trained adult," for Tommy and I alone could interpret "Mommy go bye bye yellow park" and "Apple all gone li'l movie."

At almost three, Claire seems to be where I was mid-year in the Czech Republic. I remember listening desperately, grasping one word in the flux, and from that constructing what the conversation was likely about (Claire: "Did you say 'candy,' Mama?") or learning a few phrases that seemed adequate for a number of replies and would make me seem more proficient than I was (I had "That's true of everybody" and "That will give me a hangover"; Claire has "What a bummer" and "I'm out of here"). There's even the same element of bluffing, when you guess what someone is talking about and act accordingly. I remember one day when Claire was demanding an entire bag of marshmallows. I kept telling her she could have only one.

"No," she yelled, "I want six! I want eight-fourteen! I want twenty-thirty!"

"Claire," I said firmly, "listen to Mommy. You can have one, or you can have none. You choose. One or none."

Delightedly she yelled, "I'll have none! I'll have none!"

Speaking of language, Claire is calling me—

Lots of love,
Beth Ann

April 11, 2004
Dear One,

The long spring here is lovely. Every afternoon there's a quick and dramatic thunderstorm full of pyrotechnics and big winds, very tropical. It's not that all-day drizzle that used to depress me the months I lived in London—it's over shortly and leaves the world spit-shined, twinkling. The golden sun shines through the budding leaves, and because the new leaves are such a pale green, the light that filters to the ground is a buttery chartreuse and languorous. I like best to be on the balcony of City Grocery around six with a gin and tonic and feel the long pink fingers of the sunset reach across the lengthening sky.

Tommy's out of town and last night there was such a lightning storm that Claire woke, yelling. I carried her into my bed, which I try not to do often, telling her this was a special treat, but not telling her the treat really was all mine. "Is volcanoes going to burn me with hot lava?" she asked. I reassured her, snuggled around her warm little body, and in the dark felt her small hands stroking my cheeks and eyelids. "Mama," she sighed, "my mama." Then we both slept. In the morning, we made pancakes studded with chocolate chips forming the letter C. Later, I opened the front door and found a surprise on my welcome mat. Do you remember that we live just a few blocks from the cemetery where Faulkner is buried? Well, some plastic flowers had been blown from a grave in the storm and found my front door:

white plastic carnations outlining red plastic carnations, spelling "MOM."

Concerning our Quest for Equitable Parenting—I've got a good one: the emperor penguin. Do you know about these guys? Black-backed, white-tummied, a toucan-orange stripe on their black beaks and the same orange in a big spot on either side of their heads, like Tennessee Volunteer fans wearing earmuffs.

Here's how they do it: the female incubates the egg, and she lays it, but that's the end of her shift. She uses her stubby little flippers to nudge it toward her mate, who wriggles it into a pouch at the bottom of his body so the tip of the egg rests on the tops of his feet. Then the mother, being hungry enough to eat everything in the ocean, waddles and belly-slides across the tundra and makes her big splash. She's out to sea for about two months.

During this time the real cold sweeps in, way below freezing, I mean it's cold even for Antarctica. And it's not just cold—it's black, black as the blackest place in the world, black both day and night, inseparably black, the sun never cresting the horizon, even the blizzards that assault the penguins' faces are black with black and unreflecting snow. And this whole time daddy emperor keeps the egg in the pouch, balanced on his feet, and because of this he can't move very much, so he lives off his fat, growing slowly thinner through the long black days.

With the females off feasting on salty, silvery fish, the males form tight circles, and these friendships are lifesavers, literally.

Huddled together for warmth, humped back against humped back, they duck their heads in the freezing sleet, shifting from foot to foot. Then—formal as a player being substituted in a soccer game—one penguin leaves the icy perimeter and waddles deeper into the warm, protected center, while another penguin from the center waddles to the edge for his turn as windbreaker.

Finally the eggs hatch on their fathers' feet. When the females sense it's time, they beach themselves, flopping and flippering onto the ice, shaking off the sea, and begin searching for their families. But it's still too dark to see a flipper in front of your face, so they hunt by voice. The males call and call as loudly as they can, beaks raised, flippers rigid with effort, calling and calling and calling. And the females circle and hone until they find their mates. After an affectionate reunion full of patting and nuzzling, the father gently deposits the chick on the mother's feet. And then—fair is fair—the males go off on their own fishing vacation.

What do you think of that?

Love,
BA

April 12, 2004
Dear Kathleen,

Make no mistake: motherhood is a shitty business, literally. It's amazing how much attention you'll pay to their diaper changes, the consistency, frequency, and color, you will discuss these matters with your husband, you will discuss them at meals no less. There are no bodily fluids that you won't come to know, they will sneeze on you and pee on you and vomit on you, they will have colds and raise the glazed donuts of their faces to your face and you will kiss them and you will taste their snot.

Our little family is deep in doo-doo now, having succeeded at the first part of potty-training, determined to finish the second part before Claire's third birthday. Now even more household talk revolves around this fascinating activity. No bedtime is complete without at least a few readings of *Everybody Poops* and *Sara's Potty*. And we're making progress. But this afternoon, a dirty diaper. Okay, no problem. I was cleaning Claire with the hand wipe, telling her to let me know the next time she has that "funny feeling," when something I was wiping didn't quite wipe away. I looked closer—a thin, whitish piece of thread was coming from her bottom. No time for squeamishness: I pinched the end and pulled—like a magician pulling scarves from her sleeve, out and out and out I tugged the string from the tiny starburst of her anus. Then I remembered how, yesterday, when I was flossing my teeth my little monkey watched, rapt, and the phone rang. I laid the dental floss on the edge of the sink, but when I came back it was gone . . .

Love,
Beth Ann

April 13, 2004
Dear One,

Tommy left this morning for a writers' conference in North Carolina, so Claire and I are going to make calzone for dinner—I have the dough proofing in the kitchen. It makes a huge floury mess of the countertops, but Claire loves to help knead the dough, then roll it out into a circle, place her cheese and mushrooms on half, then crimp the edges . . . if only she enjoyed the eating as much as the making. Sometimes I can't believe how little she needs to fuel that continually moving body.

You know, I'm a better mother when Tommy's out of town. It's taken me a while to realize that, but it's true. I stop looking for my relief pitcher to step in and so I relax, enjoy the game more. When we're all home, we of course have some family activities and meals together, but soon enough we're dividing the labor, because there's so very much of it. So one of us is writing, and one is with Claire. Then we switch. One of us gets her down for the nap, and the other for the night. Both of us try to lose ourselves in work when we can, even as we hear the seconds clucking their tongues as they march by. When I'm on Claire duty and Tommy's writing with his office door closed and headphones on, I end up feeling antsy for my turn, though he's very fair. But if I know Tommy's gone and no turn is coming my way, I am able to give myself over to her. There's less anxiety.

I know Tommy and I are lucky because our teaching jobs only require us to be in the classroom about six hours a week, with maybe another six to ten of conferences, advising, and committees. We can do the bulk of class prep and grading at home. And we both do our writing at home. Tommy's working on a new novel and I'm about one-third through another book of poems. Overall, our days are much more integrated than for the average couple, for we can switch back and forth between work and play, and we get to roll around with Claire a lot. Yet it's also true that there's never a time when we can feel like work is truly over, when I can be fully a mommy without feeling like I should be working, at least a little—except when I'm the sole caregiver, or Claire is sick, for then I release myself from guilt.

I read about a study in which mothers rated themselves as to how satisfied they were with their performance as mothers. Women who stayed home viewed themselves as successful mothers, as you might imagine. Women who worked full-time outside the home also felt confident in their mothering abilities. But women who worked part- or full-time from home while raising children were the most critical, on both counts—they were dissatisfied with themselves as workers and as mothers. I understand this, for sure. Don't get me wrong, I wouldn't change my situation—while I'd love a semester off, I can't imagine giving up teaching permanently (or being able to afford it). Giving up poetry? One might as well give up eating. Equally impossible is the idea of hiring a full-time nanny to care for Claire. Yet in trying to feed both my career and my daughter's imagination, I hold myself to standards I can't meet. I think of my favorite fiction writers (Virginia Woolf and Flannery O'Connor) and favorite poets (Marianne Moore and Elizabeth Bishop)—all childless. Then I think of the champion stay-at-home moms who make homemade Play-Doh and teach their six-month-olds sign language. I want membership in both groups. Is that desire nothing more than crass competition? Wouldn't it be healthier to adjust my standards?

Hmm, I'm picking up this letter again after getting the calzone in the oven. Mine has artichokes, asiago cheese, tomatoes, and pesto, yum. I'll clean the kitchen after Claire goes to bed. She's threatening to make a pasta necklace for Daddy so I might as well wait until the damage is done. I have NPR playing in the kitchen, and I just heard something that would amuse you. It seems that botanists are designing "sixty-mile-an-hour flowers." No longer is a blossom's perfume or subtle texture a selling point, for people no longer stroll through their gardens. They whip past them in cars and value the hybrids that can be appreciated from that distance at that speed. I think of my favorite flower, the slender lily of the valley, blossom of the month of May, in which both Claire and I were born, blossom I wanted to carry in my wedding bouquet, but it was three dollars a stem. When I think of that flower I think first of its scent, something antique, almost musty about it, like a grandmother's handkerchief, very floral notes, underneath them a finish of champagne. After recollecting its scent, I think of its small white fluted blossoms dangling down the stalk, which looks like a rack of skirts for pixies. And I feel sad that it won't be grown so often as, say, the new canna lily hybrids, taller, thicker, with almost fluorescent blooms, absolutely scentless. I've been reading Dorothy Wordsworth's journal on and off this week and I can't help wondering what she would make of this news story. She believed that one should walk everywhere because riding in a carriage made the scenery pass too quickly to be appreciated.

K, did you hear that two scientists from Norway are investigating ways to speed up the ten-month gestation period the baby spends in the womb? I can't believe they'll be successful. I guess I hope they won't be. A "speed pregnancy" would be hard to resist. Even if today you'd have the strength to choose the whole forty weeks, there comes a day when any pregnant woman just wants to unzip the fat suit. Imagine getting pregnant and birthing, say, three months later—I think it would be like poor Dorothy Wordsworth flying the Concorde. The jet lag would be too punishing. We need the full 280 days to go around the world, as "gestate" comes from *gestare*, and means not only "to carry in the uterus" but "to conceive of and develop gradually in the mind."

Oh, what a schoolteacher I've become, it's your spring break and I'm giving you Latin derivations . . . no one reading this letter would guess that last night at City Grocery I did three shots of tequila and danced to the Preacher's Kids.

Love,
BA

April 18, 2004
Dear One,

Last night Tommy and I watched a videotape of Claire learning to crawl. Crawling is another process we telescope and revise until it fits the myth of progress, as if the baby moves linearly from sitting to crawling, but that is rarely the case, as the video reminded me. Also, we think of infancy as a time free of frustrated desires, but the baby who decides to crawl to the shiny gum wrapper becomes obsessed with doing so, no matter the obstacle. It's amazing that a creature so small can be such a creative engineer.

First, Claire would be on her tummy and push against her feet so her butt would lift in the air. From this position she'd shuffle her feet and shove her head and shoulders along the carpet, like a polar bear scratching his neck. The next phase involved her straightening her arms, like a yogi in Downward Dog. But instead of alternating her arms, she'd jump and land, usually propelled backwards. Next, she added the right-left elbow heave, like a commando crawling under barbed wire. Finally she coordinated the alternating knees with the alternating hands, and began crawling, and wouldn't stop. She'd spy a Pizza Hut circular that had fallen from my newspaper, and she'd crawl to it, but as she reached, she'd lose her balance and fall, like a runner sliding into first.

Her sweet soft body which until then hadn't withstood any more friction than being toweled dry was now scouring itself back and forth against the carpet. And while I was proud of her, I saw her ankles grow red and scuffed and her knees start to bleed, but there was no stopping her. Finally when I couldn't stand it any longer I'd gather her into my arms and still her tiny limbs. She'd wriggle in my lap to be set down, at first. Slowly she'd calm, and I'd feel beneath my thumb pads her rabbit heart grow steady. Then, at last, she'd be dozing in my arms, worn out. Oh sweet

Claire, how I wish I could have you that small in my lap again for just one more milk-breathed nap.

Love,
Beth Ann

April 21, 2004
Dear One,

Tommy and I took Claire to a magic show, and although all of the five- and six-year-olds were into it, she wasn't impressed—she stared level-eyed at the levitating lady with only the slightest bit of wonder, my not-quite-three-year-old cynic. Later it occurred to me that perhaps she's too young to be impressed by a magic show because to her every day is a magic show—she thinks she can levitate and fly, too, or will tomorrow. Perhaps what I mistook for cynicism is merely her belief in a world without gravity or logic.

I remember how a year ago she would sit in her high chair, toss her spoon over the edge, say "uh-oh," and grab the edge of her tray to lean over and spy the spoon. I'd pick it up and hand it back to her. She'd toss it over the edge, say "uh-oh," and grab the edge of her high tray to spy it again. She'd continue to do this, endlessly fascinated, as long as I was willing to pick up the spoon, and the game never bored her because she was never sure how the spoon (or her mother) would react. She hadn't yet acquired "object permanence," the belief that just because you don't see something doesn't mean it isn't there. At a spiritual level, I hope she never does.

Claire lives in a world where markers really are magic, where there's a woset in her closet, where blue and yellow paint swirl to form a green she'd never have predicted, where an apple cut one way reveals a star, and cut the transverse way reveals the face of an owl. So the faraway black-suited man pulls a rabbit from his hat; so what? She could pull a swimming pool, or a T. rex, if they'd just pass her the hat.

Love,
Beth Ann

April 26, 2004
Dear One,

Came across a bit of a poem that seems part of our conversation about the magic of childhood. It's by Deborah Digges, whom I've never met but will read with next month at the Odyssey Bookstore in South Hadley, Mass., when I go out East to hang with my old college roommates. This quote is from "The Little Book of Hand Shadows":

> You who began inside of me,
> see a tortoise, a stork, a wolf come out of my hand.
>
> Stand behind me, your shadow eclipsing
> my shadow.
>
> Make the cock crow by opening and closing two fingers.
> We can be anyone now.

Lovely, no?
BA

April 29, 2004
Dearest K,

Just came home to your letter in which you said you've entered your second trimester and have started to show. Congratulations! Though it's true that keeping the secret with your husband those giddy early weeks is undeniably sweet. I love the way it makes you feel linked, telepathic in a group, exchanging glances when Gerber commercials air during half-time, or squeezing hands under the table when a friend asks if you plan to start a family, and you say, simply, "Soon." I bet your second trimester makes the pregnancy more concrete for Robert, because he'll be able to feel the baby kick. Tommy used to place his hands on my belly and ask, "Is that a kick? Is that one?" Later, he compared it to fishing—he kept imagining movement and doubting himself, but when a fish finally takes the line, there's no mistaking it.

It's fun that you can begin telling people. We told our mothers about our pregnancy by placing copies of the ultrasound in frames that said "I love Grandma." I told my poetry-writing students by bringing in Sylvia Plath's poem "Metaphors." It's nine lines, nine syllables per line, and lists metaphors such as "A melon strolling on two tendrils." After reading the poem, I asked the students to guess Plath's riddle. "She's pregnant," someone yelled. "Right," I said, smiling. A pause—then one by one the smiles splashed across their faces as they realized why I'd chosen that poem.

When sharing your news, you might come across some disgruntled parent-folk. You know, the kind who snort and say ruefully, "If there's anyplace you want to travel to, go now." Don't let them squelch your joy, dear K: these are the kind of people who never went anywhere *before* they had babies either.

Love,
Beth Ann

May 1, 2004
Dear One,

Prenatal Mr. Potato Head: the favorite game of expectant parents. Will she have the father's eyes, or—God help us—the great-aunt's nose? Even when the baby's born, this game continues, because the baby's looks change so much the first year. Interestingly, most babies, when they are born, slightly favor the father, but later this evens out. One theory suggests this is because the mother KNOWS the baby is hers but the father can't be completely sure, so babies who look like dad encourage bonding, which improves the baby's chances of survival. What crafty little creatures babies are. So what if they can't burp themselves.

Later, when the baby's looks even out a bit, parents entertain questions of character inheritances, which is even more interesting. Tommy and I love to discuss Claire's personality, both claiming credit for her good traits, of course. Some of her qualities are hard to pin down to any source, however. For example, Tommy and I were both fairly shy children, but Claire is incredibly dramatic, which is sometimes a bit exhausting but mostly entertaining. The other day she was outside playing on the swing set and got too close to the edge of the platform. "Claire," Tommy warned, "be careful or you'll fall off the edge, and it will hurt." "Yes," she said, "and then you will say, 'Oh my poor dead child.' "

A good story about inheritance concerns the Russian novelist Vladimir Nabokov. Nabokov read synesthetically—that is, while reading he transposed sensory impressions, like "tasting" a symphony or "hearing" a color. Once, in a friend's apartment, Nabokov picked up a novel, read a short passage in it, and proclaimed, "Cherry. A cherry-flavored book." And of another novel, "This passage is salty and sharp like barbed wire."

Nabokov's son inherited his father's gift for synesthesia. Many years after his father had died, the son visited the same apartment. The friend pulled out the original book for Nabokov's son, who'd never heard of his father's evaluation. The son read a few pages, slapped the book shut, and said, with a nod, "Cherry."

Love,
Beth Ann

May 5, 2004
Dear One,

I always knew I'd want to be a good mother to my child. What I couldn't know is that sometimes it's hard to figure out what good mothering is. Here's my dilemma for the first week of summer vacation: Claire hates her swim lessons. I've paid for five, and we've done two, the second even more traumatic than the first. Should I make her stick it out in the hopes that she'll grow to like swimming, and to teach her not to quit? Or should I capitulate, say we're done with the pool, take her out for ice cream, and enjoy her relieved affection while showing her I'm responsive to her fears and limitations?

I should have guessed she'd hate the lessons; I, too, hate swimming. But I don't want Claire to be the only child that can't swim, don't want to risk a drowning, so I let her pick out the most rufflybottomed swimsuit in the children's store and signed her up for a week of instruction. The first day, sweet gorgeous Kristin, the lifeguard at the public pool, coached Claire to "make a monkey face." Claire would hold her breath in puffed-out cheeks. Then Kristin would glide Claire, face submerged, in the water. Claire would surface, spluttering, de-monkeyfied, crying, "No more under water. All done." But Kristin persevered. Soon she'd have tricked another monkey face out of Claire and we'd rinse, repeat, rinse, repeat, like shampoo.

Yesterday morning, Claire asked hopefully, "No swimming

today?" "Claire, it will be fun," I lied. If anything, it was worse. She gave little hiccuping sobs between submersions, begged me with bluish lips to get her out and towel her dry, while all around her children cannonballed fearlessly into the water.

This morning, the first words she said upon waking were "No swimming today." And for hours she repeated this like a mantra. She was terrified, and I was more than ready for a new topic of conversation. Maybe it wasn't worth it. It began to rain and I was glad to postpone the decision until tomorrow. To cheer her up, I decided to stroll Claire to the library (she loves to, one by one, feed the books into the metal book drop). We passed the pool halfway to the library and I saw Kristin reopening the pool as the sun had returned. Through the chain-link fence we discussed possible makeup times. And then as I started to wheel Claire away, she erupted into a howl. She'd changed her mind and wanted to swim. I tried to explain that it was too late, that we'd missed our time, Claire didn't have a suit on, Kristin had a new lesson starting up, etc. Nothing helped. Finally I just pushed the stroller to the library and back with Claire screaming the entire time, kicking her legs, a bona fide red-faced tantrum, people craning from their porches to glimpse Unfit Mother Abusing Innocent Child.

Only after I got her home and she'd tattled to Tommy— "Mommy wouldn't let me" (sob) "swim with Miss Kristin" (sob)—could I slowly soothe her, a little apple juice, her stuffed bunny, a back rub, the Wiggles video, and gradually her terrible chest-heavings grew further apart, then softened to a voiced inhale, and then quieted, the way an overheated car engine clicks itself cool. The rest of the evening, her little face was tear-swollen. She was subdued, clingy, and almost unbearably sweet, kissing my kneecaps as she belly-slid off the couch or hugging my leg as I talked on the phone. She was so exhausted that she actually asked to be put to bed. After I tucked her in, her sleepy voice trailed me down the hall: "No swimming tomorrow, Mommy?"

I don't know what caused Claire's sudden determination to swim. I don't know what I'll do about her lesson tomorrow. I don't know, I realize daily, how to be the perfect mom. I'm making mistakes, but there's no answer key. Sometimes I think the most I can hope for is to observe her closely enough that I can at least make different mistakes next time.

What I want to take away from this: when Claire throws a fit, I need to remember that she hates it as much as I do. She doesn't want to lose control as she does when her limbs are flailing, her screams rising, her eyes stinging with tears. If she could stop herself, she would. I need to remind myself of that, instead of focusing on my own frustration, or embarrassment, or, more rarely, amusement. These little people are capable of the same emotions we are, the same terror and rage. Even when I see the cause for her emotions as trivial, the passion in her emotions is real, and the costs are also real, the exhaustion and remorse. I need to be respectful of this, respond in a way that dignifies her.

Dear K, I'm beginning to realize that one reason I enjoy advising you is I get to advise myself at the same time.

Love,
Beth Ann

May 8, 2004
Dear One—

I am glad to know you read my last letter to your tummy. I like to think of your baby receiving its first letter from me, lounging on the red velvet recamier of your womb. Perhaps its little ears were pressed against the tortellini of your belly button and it heard the thrum of your voice sounding my words, felt the whoosh of your lungs expand and deflate, pillows around its buoyant body. Do you know that the infant's heartbeat slows when it hears its mother's voice? What power we harbor. Even when they are curled in the womb, that original installation art, we possess the ability to calm them. Oh those little gravity-free astronauts, tethered to the mother ship, comfortable upside down or sideways or anyways at all. I have an amazing ultrasound picture of Claire with her arms behind her head, her legs stretched out as if my pelvis was her hammock, which, I suppose, it was. Of course that endearing pose is exactly why I got into such trouble delivering Claire—because she tried to come out with her arms behind her head and they got stuck. So I had to push her elbows, shoulders, and head out at the same time. But that, darling, is a story for another day.

Sweet Kathleen, this morning's mail brought your letter in which you compare my scribblings to you to Rilke's *Letters to a Young Poet*. I adore that book too, am awed at Rilke's passion and wisdom. And his generosity—imagine crafting such eloquent letters to a young writer he'd never even met! While it's true as you point out that I'm the age Rilke was when writing the last of the letters, the comparison ends there, I'm afraid. Rilke was such a good guide to young Mr. Kappus and all you have is me, and there's so much I haven't told you yet and perhaps won't be able to before October 28 and then you'll be too busy to write or read many letters. I started paging through my copy of *Letters to a Young Poet* and now feel a little shy to write to you, and disdainful with myself for not being a better advisor. Sigh. I'll close with a favorite passage from Rilke:

"Be patient toward all that is unsolved in your heart and to try to love the questions themselves like locked rooms and like books that are written in a very foreign tongue . . . They are difficult things with which we have been charged; almost everything serious is difficult, and everything is serious."

Love,
Beth Ann

May 15, 2004
K,

Sometimes when Claire passes out of one or another of her cute stages and I get anxious about her getting older, I think of the waiter in London's Chinatown and grow calm again.

We'd just come out of a long matinee at the theater, and we were very hungry, and I was three months pregnant. We wandered among the crowded neon joints, then chose a restaurant down an alley, behind the main drag. The restaurant's sign wasn't translated into English. We pulled open the oversized red door and stepped inside. It was dark, and there were no customers. We would have turned around and slipped back into the fading day, but already the smiling, bowing waiter was gesturing toward a russet banquette where we should sit. We couldn't read the menu, and the solicitous waiter could tell. "I bring?" he asked, and we nodded.

After a few minutes, the waiter brought the first dish. As he set it down steaming on the table, he promised "more coming," and disappeared. Who knows what it was called, pork and fried scallions in a tangy sauce, unbelievably delicious. He came back after another few minutes, picked up the empty plate, and set down a new dish of something marvelous, promising again "more coming." I think he was concerned that we'd fill up before we'd sampled all the piquant riches he could ferry from the kitchen doorway, masked by prodigious greenery. As he removed each empty plate, I felt a pang thinking I'd never know what the dish was called or perhaps even eat it again—but suddenly there would be an intriguing new dish in front of me, bathing my face in steam. No worry, he told us. More coming. More coming.

Love,
Beth Ann

May 19, 2004
Dear One,

Thank you for the Inuit doll for Claire's birthday—it's gorgeous, right down to the tiny hand-sewn leather boots. Claire loves it and has painted a thank-you card, but as it's still drying I'll send my own thanks first.

This morning I marked her height as a new three-year-old on the lime-green wall of her bedroom. If I hadn't held the pencil in my own hand, I'd never have believed the mark once she stepped away. The height chart is like a magic beanstalk. It makes me think of what Virginia Woolf said—we hurtle through life so quickly that we should visualize ourselves "with our hair flying back like the tail of a horse."

Now Claire's napping with the Inuit doll tucked under her elbow. In the backyard two handymen are setting up a wooden jungle gym for her birthday present—I can't wait until she wakes and sees it. We've got her birthday party at the park tomorrow afternoon, and we've already made up the treat bags and stuffed the Nemo piñata. No plans tonight except for our pal David coming over for a late dinner al fresco. Until then, I have a lovely afternoon to write to you. I'm sitting on the patio with my iced coffee and the Thin Mints my Girl Scout neighbor Amanda just dropped by.

Girl Scouts now have it easy, judging from Amanda's uniform. They *iron* the badges on their sashes. Were you ever a Girl Scout? In my time (I turn thirty-three next week, and have begun using phrases like "in my time"—one of the consolations of aging), we sewed our patches on. Truth is, I wouldn't have had it any other way. The zenith of my week was the closing of our Wednesday meeting when my scout leader would retrieve the shipment of badges. I would wait for mine with cupped palms, like a supplicant receiving the communion host. Then I'd pedal my bike home and hurry upstairs to my mother's closet to excavate her sewing kit from the clutter of shoes and handbags. Sitting on the closet floor, with even, nearly invisible stitches I'd sew the patch into place, making sure my handiwork was as neat from the back as the front. And I'd live for the next Wednesday when I could show off the sash, like a sorority sister eager to flash the engagement ring she scored over spring break.

The patches common to every scout—the wings that signified flying up from Brownies to Girl Scouts, the rainbow connoting the bridge to junior Girl Scouts, the Girl Scout identity strip and Council identity strip that, stacked, looked like the halves of a hamburger bun—didn't captivate me. I sewed them on, sure, but what I craved—Catholic school girl, honor student, chronic pleaser—was external verification of internal merit, those half-dollar circles sewn three to a row (right beneath the Cookie Activity Pins), each proving the mastery of some skill. I was, officially, a Model Citizen and Earth Lover and Horse Rider and Pen Pal. I had Money Sense. I knew Pet Care and First Aid and Caring for Children. I was all over Ceramics & Clay. Let's Get Cooking was not just an expression to me; Collecting Hobbies was something I'd indeed collected. Yarn & Fabric Arts? *No problemo*. I can still macramé a mean plant holder.

Rows of badges filled the front of my sash and then marched up the back in tidy formation. As the months rolled into years, I earned all of the easy patches and many of the tougher ones— even some for skills I had no interest in—grimly checking off requirements for Car Care and Science Sleuth and Math Whiz and Ms. Fix It. Naturally, my acquisition rate slowed down. Soon, whole months passed before I would fetch Mom's sewing kit.

And finally there came a point when I realized I had gotten all of the patches I was going to get. It was, I admitted, unlikely that I would be a Girl Scout in a foreign country, thereby earning International Friendship. And though I eagerly scanned the pool for a drowning child each time I went, Life Saver seemed destined to elude.

Which is why, one sunny Wednesday in October of my eighth-grade year, I quit. My parents were shocked. They'd had visions, I'm sure, of Girl Scout scholarships to college and a lifetime supply of Do-Si-Dos. *But you love Girl Scouts!* they protested. Silly parents.

So that's the type of kid I was, and that's the type of mother I have to struggle not to be. Because that eager patch-earner still lurks in me, Girl Scout Guide in hand, pencil behind ear. And while being a Model Citizen might help in certain places, like airport security or bake sales, it's not the most practical training for the wild territory of motherhood.

As a teenager I imagined, as all teenagers do, that I'd perfect the art of adulthood. I knew I'd get an A. I'd have nearly invisible stitches. I was a late bloomer in terms of rebellion—only in my junior year in London did I discover all I'd been missing by not squeezing the toothpaste in the middle. My newly emerging identity as a poet gave me permission to stick out, practice courage. Not that I was good at poetry—I was imitative and restrained. And I was as grimly determined to direct a poem as I had been a decade earlier to earn my badges. While I didn't write outlines, I steered each poem resolutely to the message I wanted to get across to the reader. No bathroom breaks! No detours! No stopping for 72-ounce steaks, free if eaten in under an hour!

It wasn't really until my first year at the University of Arkansas that I began to see how tidy and corrupt my poetry was. The poet Jack Gilbert visited the M.F.A. program, and we had a conference. After reading several of my poems, he told me a story. It went like this: in Amsterdam, because of the many curving roads, sudden canals, and one-way bridges, it's difficult to get to know the city. So difficult, in fact, that it takes a taxi driver five years to earn a license. Because of this, sometimes there's a taxi shortage. Once, said Jack, the shortage got so severe that the city came up with a plan: a passenger could take one of the regular black taxis, pay full fare, and get to the destination speedily. Or, a passenger could take one of the new red taxis-in-training. These taxis were cheaper, but when you got in one, you never quite knew what you were in for. You'd get to your destination, sure, but you might take a few wrong turns, might get a little lost. Who knew what you might see along the way.

After telling me this, Jack Gilbert paused. "Beth Ann," he said, "take the red taxi."

In my next poem, I stopped steering. The poem took a detour and ended at a destination I didn't even know I knew. It was fun. I tried it again. And gradually I learned to give up control. To, sometimes, at night, on a country hill, take my hands off the wheel and turn the headlights off just for the prickly thrill of it. There's an old workshop adage that still holds a lot of truth for me: "No surprise for the writer, no surprise for the reader." I was surprised by what I contained, by what we all contain. What mysterious creatures we humans be.

Around the same time I was learning to let my poems discover what they wanted to say, I was falling in love with cowboy-booted, country-talking Tommy, at Arkansas to study fiction. And he did his part to mellow out the Girl Scout badge-earner, who, after all, was a rather unhappy little overachiever. Being with Tommy softened me. Love can do that. I went from being an anti-TV, near-vegetarian, cultural snob to a woman who would spend Saturday mornings in bed with Tommy watching *Cheers* reruns and eating BBQ while he stroked my hair. Also, all the anger I'd been stoking inside myself and directing at men—anger that stemmed from my father's alcoholism and sordid death— puttered out in the fresh wind of his loyalty and affection.

Looking back, I see how both poetry and love prepared me for raising Claire. The Girl Scout I'd been would have cracked after a month of motherhood. One can't grimly check off the requirements and bump the child from stage to stage. There's so much instinct involved, so much trial and error. Everything is contextual and often cloudy. I establish a rule about Claire eating at least a bite of each different food on her plate, for example, and try to stick to it—then one day she's sick or upset and I see what she really needs is to feel she has a little control over her fate, is able to say "no" and have Mommy listen. I've learned to let her be messy and silly, because it's a way of being creative. Learned to let her put the black stripes on the orange-frosted Nemo birthday cupcakes, even if that means no party guest will discern the shape of a fish. I've learned to watch and react to her, instead of steering her to the conclusion that I preordained best.

I signed Claire up for Kindermusik when she was a year old because she's always been musical, always loved to sing and clap. But she was the youngest one in the class by several months and didn't have the motor skills necessary for some of the songs. Also, she didn't have the maturity yet to wait like the older children for her turn at the zither. The Kindermusik teacher spoke sharply to Claire when it was time to crawl like a bear and Claire was still hopping like a kangaroo. I began to sense the teacher didn't like Claire, perhaps didn't like children. And one week when I was getting Claire ready she said, "No go, Mommy," so we didn't, and we forfeited our fees (and our graduation diploma!), and Claire and I stayed home banging pots and pans with wooden spoons to our raucous delight. I can't always take the red taxi with Claire, but I've learned there are times she needs me to. Times when we both need to.

Ah, poetry and love—you found me and prepared me, you drilled me on the skills of ingenuity and risk taking, and so you readied me for the radical nature of motherhood. Motherhood, for you I gave up guarantees and road maps, for you I traded my plaid uniform skirt for a cardboard rocket ship. For you, I have appeared indecorous, and, more than once, worse than indecorous. Yes, I have been downright foolish. And it would seem you give so little in return—no patches! No gold stars! Not even a sash! I cannot fully predict or perfect you (I believe it, I am almost thirty-three, old enough to play with phrases like "in my time"), I will spend my life attempting it, and I will fail, I will fail because I know that ten lifetimes aren't enough. And that is both my sorrow and my deep, thrumming joy.

Love,
Beth Ann

May 22, 2004
Dear One,

We just finished dinner and the last of Claire's leftover birthday cake, and I'm back inside after admiring my new garden—today I planted flowers that my friends gave me at a little birthday luncheon. Because my birthday is just three days away from Claire's, I tend to overlook it in the excitement over "pin-the-fin-on-Dory." How sweet my friends are for insisting on a celebration. And truthfully I'm just selfish enough to have felt a bit blue if my day passed without any fuss. After they treated me to lunch, we walked outside the restaurant, and the back of Blair's wagon was loaded with butterfly bushes, zinnias, and mandevilla, because I'd said some months ago that I wanted to learn to garden this summer.

It's tropically hot here already. Playing with Claire on her new swing set before dinner, we got attacked by the season's first mosquitoes. I took her back inside to rub calamine lotion on her polka-dot calves, and I reflected on how the mosquitoes have always loved her the way they've always loved me, though they shun Tommy as if he's dipped in DEET. And then I recalled one night in her infancy finally getting her to sleep and gently placing her in the basinet in the darkened nursery. Letting out the breath I didn't know I'd been holding, because it seemed to take: she hadn't wakened. But then I heard the tinny sound of a mosquito insisting itself somewhere nearby. Dilemma—if I turned on the light to find it and kill it, she'd awaken. If I didn't, it would bite her. So I shucked my nightshirt over my head and held my arms out, waited for the shrill whine to stop as the mosquito sank his needle into my warm flesh. It only took a second. As I waited I caught a shadowy glimpse of myself in the moonlit half-moon mirror above Claire's changing table and grinned at my grandiloquent notion that my outstretched arms made me look crucified.

Love,
Beth Ann

June 2, 2004
Dear One—

I'm sorry, sweet pal, it's been a week since I've written. I took
my trip out East, first to give a reading and then to have Wild
Women's Weekend IV, the annual gathering of my old college
roommates—every year we pick a new place and this time we
chose Newport, Rhode Island.

I've moved around enough that I've come to value more and
more these friends that go back fifteen years now. When we get
together, we're able to move so quickly to deep levels of conversation. We don't need to fill each other in on backstory—we
know each other's parents, siblings, and ex-boyfriends, and now
we know each other's husbands and children. On Saturday afternoon, after some shopping, we stopped by the liquor store and
bought some red wine, then got in our bathing suits and wedged
ourselves in the hot tub like pie pieces in Trivial Pursuit. We
drank and we laughed and we talk, talk, talked. It did me a world
of good. Those weekends are a spa trip for the emotions, and we
all leave with insight into our concerns—should Laura and Andy
go into business for themselves? Should Denise worry if she and

Scott aren't sure they want children? I talked with my roomies about our second-baby-or-not dilemma and felt more peaceful afterward. That night I dreamt that I was back in the hot tub and my friends put their hands on my stomach and I felt a baby kick, and I woke happy.

Your letter of May 11 asks about finding out the baby's gender— I think there are good arguments for both sides. There's something pure about not knowing, trusting the mystery and the way things have been done since the first stirrings came from inside of us, the original cave drawings being the tiny fists pressing into the velvety red walls. (Once, I saw Claire's hand the size of a quarter outstretched against the skin of my belly so that I could count the fingers—then that star was sucked back into its own universe.)

As for me, I had to have a lot of ultrasounds and tests because my previous baby miscarried. I started out not wanting to know, but finally, propped there with the midwife and nurses and technicians leaning over me as if it were winter and I a potbellied stove, I felt it seemed stubborn to make them keep choosing gender neutral pronouns.

I really wanted a daughter and was overjoyed to hear I was carrying one—in fact, it had occurred to me that perhaps I should find out the gender to work up enthusiasm if the baby was a boy. And knowing allowed for a more personal welcome for the newborn—it's nice when you can say "Feel her kick" to your husband, instead of "Feel it." And we could address her by the name we'd chosen. Claire, Claire, Claire, how I never get tired of saying that word. And I began a pregnancy journal. Tommy took a picture of my belly each month and I pasted it inside, along with little wishes I had for Claire. I'd tell her about gifts she received, or mention what music I played her, or describe her kicks (I've read that a baby can kick hard enough to crack the mother's rib, and after Claire's gestation, I don't doubt it). And we decorated the nursery—I glazed the ceiling sky blue, and with the glaze still wet, rubbed off some cloudy circles with rags made from Tommy's old T-shirts, making a ceiling of sky for that sweet child to gaze on in the rare early moments when her eyes were open at all. I didn't know then of course that we'd be moving to Mississippi when Claire was two months old. I often think of that nursery and wonder if that sky shines on another child now, or if it's been painted over in some terribly tasteful cream.

Ultimately, Kathleen, I think you will be happy with whatever you and Robert decide. And, sadly, whatever you decide will probably fetch some criticism. One of the really strange things I've come to learn about the culture of motherhood is that it's very judgmental. The harshest critics of mothers are other mothers. I'm not sure why this is so—perhaps because expectant mothers receive so much hysteria-tinged advice that we feel paranoid ("Before every single bite of food you put in your mouth, ask yourself, 'Is this *really* the best thing for my baby?' " one book recommended—shortly before I hurled it across the living room). So perhaps we've grown so confused and doubtful of our own instincts and abilities that we cling fiercely to the idea that our decisions are right—which must mean all other decisions are wrong.

What helps me calm my fears and mute my criticisms is viewing our child rearing through the lens of history. We don't have to go back very far to see that our rigid standards for prenatal care are rather recent. Many in my generation had mothers who smoked and drank throughout pregnancy. My friend Katrina told me her mom went into labor during a Stroh's Brewery tour! Even today, advice for expectant moms varies enormously from country to country. Frenchwomen aren't told to avoid Brie or reduce their alcohol. Italian women aren't told to cut down on caffeine, though their weight is monitored closely. British women are told they can have up to eight drinks a week, but to avoid peanuts and peanut butter. My Irish friend said that the first thing they brought her in the Dublin hospital after she gave birth was a pint of Guinness, "to help her milk come in." We could decide to be confused or overwhelmed by these variations—or decide that there is a range of ways to grow a healthy baby. Trust the decisions that you and Robert make, and don't judge yourself (or other new mothers) too harshly.

Love,
Beth Ann

June 5, 2005
Dear K,

I'm reading the most marvelous book, *Journal of a Solitude* by May
Sarton. I bought it because my friend Linda said it helped her during her divorce. So I decided to get one for dear Amber, as her
divorce wobbles along like a wheel off a bike. While I was waiting
at the Square Books counter for it to be wrapped, I started peeking
inside, scanning a paragraph or two, and soon I was surrendering,
climbing the stairs to the café and buying an iced coffee, settling
down at a balcony table overlooking the square. I'll have to order
Amber a new copy, as this book needs to stay where I am, forever.

Published in 1973, it chronicles a year of Sarton's life as she
neared sixty, without a husband or children. While Sarton and I
are both female poets, we're about as different temperamentally as
can be. She's examining what it means to live alone, and I'm examining what it means never to be alone. She faces loneliness and
depression; I face losing myself in the insistent needs of others.
Her home life is centered on individual rituals that give meaning
to a life, arranging flowers, wooing birds to her feeder. My home
life is almost devoid of ritual, each day an improvisation, the house
noisy with friends and houseguests, and all of it a moveable feast,
the dazzle of travel always a few days or weeks away.

We're perfect foils, Sarton and I. She writes, "Am I too old to
acquire the knack for happiness?" I claim the opposite worry. I
wonder if I'm like Browning's Duchess of Ferrara, "too easily

impressed." Not rigorous enough with my spirit, my pilgrim's progress. Does happiness make me trivial? Oh my elation at a great pair of shoes on sale! My delight in dressing up, dining out, drinking too much wine, flirting with the waiter. Tommy would say, I know, not to change; these are things he loves about me. Well, I wouldn't change *that* about *him*. Yet I feel in her solitude Sarton has grabbed hold of some of life's spiky truths and is courageous in a way I haven't been.

On another note—Sarton writes about "people in their thirties mourning their lost youth because we have given them no ethos that makes maturity appear an asset." I very much feel this to be true. Turning twenty-one is the nadir of American achievement; one can get smashed legally, and as there are no further milestones after that, each succeeding birthday reeks of diminishment. People start to lie about their age, as if maturity is a thing to be ashamed of. Because you turn twenty-two in a few days, perhaps these thoughts are on your mind. Well, I'm not going to say I don't miss the body I had as a teenager, the elastic belly skin that snapped back after I pinched it. Now I gawk like a pubescent boy at the ease of Claire's swim instructor in her bathing suit, the taut abs and perky chest. Yes, the body, of course I miss (predictably) the body. But that's about all I miss. Even my college years—I loved them, and I can't imagine being the person I am now without my roommates, but I wouldn't want to go back to who I was then and suffer through the same doubts and painful experiments.

And I'm not the only one who feels this way. Time and again

I've been in a group of people in their forties, fifties, and up who, when talk turns to aging, make the typical lamentations, but sometimes, later, softly, confess that they prefer their lives now, prefer themselves now. This secret is kept from those who need to hear it—the despairing young. Movies certainly don't spoil the secret—how rarely they present a middle-aged woman falling in love, for example, or living by herself in any kind of creative and productive way. What I want you to know: so far, it just gets better.

Don't open the enclosed present until your big day! I half feel like I should have gotten you something practical, for the baby, but decided that's precisely why you need something naughty and frivolous. The practical will arrive shortly: I'm sending on a box of maternity clothes as soon as I search the attic.

Love,
Beth Ann

June 8, 2004
Dear One, dear dear—

Don't worry, yes you can ask about the miscarriage. If I've seemed hesitant to talk about it, it's only because I wouldn't want to scare you. There was a time, a long time, when I couldn't talk about it. A baby died in me, I was a walking grave, and it was the dark secret I'd take to my own grave. Now I can talk about it. In fact, I want to.

Unlike some of my friends in high school and college, I always knew I wanted to be a mother. I was born for it, I felt: I made homemade yogurt, for Pete's sake! So there was never any question about if; the only question was when, as Tommy and I spent the first few years of marriage moving too often from one temporary teaching job to another. Finally, I landed the tenure-track job at Knox, and I was eager to start trying. Maybe too eager—I remember Tommy was about to go out on a book tour for *Poachers* when I realized I was ovulating. He was packing his toiletries when I cornered him and barked, "Get your pants off and get in bed! And I mean now!" Not my sexiest come-on.

Concentrating on making a baby distracted me from thinking about my father, who had just died from cirrhosis. He had been such a beautiful man and then got so sick from the drink, so sick and so crazy, and my family suffered terribly, publicly, as he left us and drank himself to death over the course of a few years in which he divorced my mother and took up with a stewardess (not in that order) and squandered all the family money, forcing my mom to sell the house she'd loved so deeply. Eventually he succeeded in dying for his great love, alcohol, in a seedy VA hospital. But instead of focusing on the withering of my family, I fastened onto the hopeful future. Yes, Tommy and I conceived a new life, and I would blossom forth. I would be great with child.

When I was just six weeks into the pregnancy, we went on a trip to New Orleans. While there, Tommy and I did a volunteer gig teaching poetry to fourth graders at an inner-city school. So I was at the board talking about using concrete words instead of abstract terms—"Can you pour gravy on it?" I asked so they could see "sad" was abstract, "sandpaper" was not—when I felt a sudden slash of wetness between my legs. I was wearing a long skirt and I put my fingers in my pocket, felt my underwear. I took my hand out of my pocket, and my fingertips were smeared with blood.

Tommy took me back to the hotel and he paged the midwife. I was crying and bleeding and whimpering on the bed. I remember a maid knocking to see if she could make up the room and Tommy roaring "NO!" at the closed door. When the midwife phoned, she said with a worried voice that I shouldn't worry—as many as 40 percent of pregnant women spot. Blood thick now on the white sheets, blood bright as Mardi Gras, more blood than I could imagine holding in my body. And cramps as if someone had grabbed a fistful of my guts and twisted. The midwife told us then that if I started passing clots of tissue—God, it is awful—to bring them in a cup to the hospital. Doctors could test if I had miscarried, or if I'd need a D&C—an abortion—to remove the remaining "fetal matter." *It's my baby*, I wanted to shout, *not fetal matter*.

The bleeding and cramping stopped, so we didn't go to the hospital, and we left New Orleans the next day. Back in Illinois, I went straight for an ultrasound. While they couldn't see the baby, they told me not to worry, because they saw a very healthy placenta, and good fluid, and also "Brandal's ring," a positive indication of pregnancy. My blood work was perfect, as were my hormone levels. So I went home consoled—everything was okay. This child was loved, and I would not allow anything to harm it. I swallowed my fears and my vitamins.

We were scheduled for a follow-up ultrasound a few weeks later, and we drove to the hospital chattering and laughing, excited to hear the baby's heartbeat. I was propped, half lying on the cot, and the technician shook a squeeze bottle, the kind you'd use for mustard, and squirted the warm gel on my belly. The midwife was there on one side of me, Tommy on the other holding my hand, and we turned expectant faces to the screen. The technician rubbed the wand all over my stomach, circling and circling, and we watched the magic mirror of the screen swirl with snow. Somewhere in that fuzzy cloud was our baby. I knew that ultrasound works by echoes, that the waves bouncing off my baby's body would form a picture. "Where's the baby?" I said, confused, thinking they must be able to read the screen in a way I couldn't. The wand pressed harder on my stomach. The technician dodged my question, dodged my eyes, the wand pressing faster its figure eights, infinities. There was no heart, no heart, no heart. The silence grew unbearable. Then I was shattering it, shrieking, "Where's my baby? Where's my baby?" And that was the only echo in the white-tiled room, four heads turned toward the blizzard on the screen, hot tears running out of my eyes into my ears as we all watched the monitor where nothing kept appearing and appearing in the gray yawning swirls of static, constellations without stars, heavens without a God.

What does it mean when you're pregnant and there's no baby? Each day that week, we sought the answer from specialists in Peoria and Iowa City who gave me vaginal ultrasounds, a condom unrolled on the wand before it was inserted. Tests, blood work, cells from my womb walls smeared between finger-long panes of glass. Finally, a doctor coming into the room where Tommy and I sat, silent, gripping hands. The doctor shutting the door behind him. We had, he believed, a rare kind of pregnancy called a "blighted ovum." He talked using his hands and choosing small words, the way you'd explain something to a scared child, which is what I was. "After the egg is fertilized," he began, "it divides, and half of the cells forms the baby, and the other half forms the baby's food and shelter, its placenta, yolk sac, etc." He went on to tell me that he believed there had been a problem with the division of the fertilized egg. The half that made the placenta was thriving, but the half that was to make the baby never developed, or never developed very far. The doctor said he couldn't give us complete assurance of this. Nor could he guarantee that there was no baby inside me, though he did say that no baby had ever been born successfully when the yolk sak was so much more developed than the fetus. He thought the best thing would be to terminate the pregnancy, but it was up to us.

"And one more thing," he said, gravely rising from his chair.

"Your ovaries look abnormal." They were enlarged, he said, and peanut-shaped. There was a possibility that I might have ovarian cancer. He wouldn't know anything definite until the pregnancy was terminated.

This was on a Thursday. The D&C was scheduled for Monday. I don't remember much about those days in between. And I don't remember being worried about the cancer. My baby was dead. Or there was no baby. I couldn't get past that to thinking about anything else.

On Monday, they gave me the D&C. On Tuesday morning, I taught my class. Near the end of the class hour, I excused myself to go to the bathroom because I was having cramps, and when I stood up from the toilet, a piece of tissue, elephant gray and rubbery, fell from my vagina onto my shoe. I know this was part of the blood-rich placenta that I'd been growing to nourish the baby. With a piece of toilet paper I picked up the shrapnel of placenta and flushed it. I washed the black leather toe of my pump at the sink and touched up my makeup in front of the mirror. Then I locked myself in the stall and wept until the building closed. I didn't tell my students, or my colleagues, or my friends. I felt I was harboring a shameful secret. I was in a brand-new town in a brand-new job and with a newly dead dad, and Tommy and I were alone in the world.

In the weeks to come, there were many follow-up visits in which it was revealed that my ovaries had shrunk to their regular size. I was assured that I could get pregnant again, although we had to wait three months before we could try. The months were made of weeks and the weeks made of days and the days made of eternities. Everything I did was spotted with reminders of the baby we didn't have. Where did we put the tiny onesies we'd already bought for the child? The plush caterpillar rattle my mom sent? I don't know. Maybe Tommy threw them away while I was teaching. My mother and Tommy's mother both said the same well-meaning thing when they heard about the blighted ovum, and about the half that was destined to become the fetus not progressing: "At least a baby didn't die." But to me of course, a baby DID die: my baby, my first love, to whom I had been reading Shakespeare's sonnets each morning. Yet I knew these two women whom I love so much were speaking kindly, reasonably.

I kept thinking about the ultrasound and the X of the technician's cursor skimming over the screen. I was reminded of how actors know to find their places on the dark stage because each has an X of fluorescent tape which shows them where to stand. But this time, the star didn't show. There was nothing. I'm upset over nothing, I kept telling myself in the weeks that followed the D&C. *At least a baby didn't die.* I thought of people I knew who'd had miscarriages late in the pregnancy. Or delivered a stillborn. My friend David had told me about the "presentation" of his stillborn child—how the doctors and nurses brought the dead infant to him and his wife in the hospital room, wrapped in a receiving blanket and wearing a thin cotton cap. Then they rolled the brim of the cap off to show the soft, crushed skull. And drew the blanket down to show the spinal column on the outside of the baby's skin. The presentation is supposed to help the couple grieve. Perhaps it does. It's the most awful thing I've heard, and when David told me, he started crying—my big-shouldered, rugby-playing friend—yet David and his wife got on with their lives. I'm weak, selfish to be so upset, I told myself. Nothing even close to that happened to you. You have nothing to be upset about, nothing.

Daytime, I blocked it out. I simply decided not to talk about the miscarriage, not even to my college roommates. That year, our Wild Women's Weekend was going to be in Portland, Maine, at Denise's house. Often in the early happy weeks of my pregnancy, I'd imagined telling the girls that I was pregnant. How they'd squeal, how we'd hug. And this was to be a special weekend indeed because both Beth and Carmen were pregnant, and we were having a shower for them. So, in my envisioning of the weekend, I'd decided we should celebrate their pregnancies the first two days, and I'd share my news with them on Sunday night, so I didn't hog the spotlight.

Instead of that happy scene, the weekend was a painful farce for me, oohing and ahhing about each little hat or blanket. Piled on the couch with my best friends, in our pajamas, eating cookie dough and drinking Bud Light, I'd never felt so lonely. They could tell something was wrong, but I didn't want to wreck the party, didn't want my pregnant pals self-conscious about their glorious bellies, the pregnancy massages and pedicures we'd treated them to at the spa in Portland. But the last night, instead of telling them about my pregnancy, I told them about my blighted ovum. And then Laura said the words that, like a key, opened me into my grieving. She said, "Whether the baby is four years old, or four minutes, it's still a death." That Laura—who'd had two sons and a miscarriage herself—could know this, could say this, allowed me to mourn that child.

In the months after the miscarriage, I had distanced Tommy, because I asked him not to talk about it, which he respected. Now I knew I needed to tell him my feelings. It wasn't easy, but when I dreamt about the baby, I'd describe the dream, his arms around my flattened stomach, the chilly Illinois dawn coming through the drapes. At first, the words came as haltingly as they did from the Tin Man in the Wizard of Oz when he'd been found rusting in the field. Gradually, the talking seemed to help. But it wasn't until a year later when I'd successfully delivered a healthy Claire that I was able to talk about the miscarriage to anyone else, or begin writing about it, which was another step in understanding my emotions.

I stopped comparing my pregnancy which ended so early to friends' stillbirths and other tragedies. I stopped trying to rank sorrow, realized that the world has sorrow enough for all of us, and when some of it falls to you the best hope you have is letting yourself suffer through it. I suffered through it. I suffer through it. I allowed myself to think of the child as exactly that, a child. It wasn't nothing; it was never nothing.

That's why it's okay for you to ask me about that death, as I've learned to think of it, and talk of it. For so long I told myself to get over it, was impatient with my weakness. But now I see it was weakness that kept me from grieving how I needed to grieve. And now I know that I'll never "get over" my miscarriage. I've stopped wanting to. I'll carry it, instead. I'll carry it and carry it and never put it down.

Love,
Beth Ann

June 10, 2004
Dear One,

This morning Claire and I were lions. We slept in a den of pillows, licked our furry paws, tongued water from a bowl, roared terrible roars, bounded outside to chase off the birds that dared to land on our vast savanna. Once outside, we circled twice in the empty kiddie pool, then settled against its sky-blue sides. When the daddy lion brought us corn on the cob, we pounced on it, snarled between bites, and laughed between snarls.

By then it was around ten and time for Tommy and me to switch Claire-care. I came to my desk to read poems while the father-daughter roars rebounded down the hallway.

You know, K, a thing I love about mothering is a thing I love about poetry: both make you a child again. Pound said famously about poetry: "Make it new." Toddlers at play make the same demand. Both disallow dead metaphors and clichés, the fossils of our language. Everything is alive with mystery and "Why is the meantime mean?" and "I have a big apple tight" and "I wear make up then make down." We are dipped in turpentine, the film is wiped from our eyeballs, we really see what we are looking at (Why do we so rarely see?). Both poetry and motherhood are humbling, they do not care whether you appear civilized to your neighbors, they are greedy, they demand you eat with your fingers, they lie in wait for the moment you announce you've got it nailed (fool!), and then it is all tantrums, or all silence. Both cost you more than you think you can bear, repay you more than you deserve. How to get the right last line, or how to get the child to eat asparagus—both are problems that repel logic, oh ridiculous limited logic. The kryptonite of creativity alone can solve them. Why should Claire eat her asparagus? Because it's the lion tamer's whip, and she doesn't want to be tamed. Naturally. "Why?" both poetry and motherhood ask, and when they receive the answer, ask "Why?" again. Both terrify us because we can't control them. "Why," they ask, "Why," they answer, "Why?"

I was asked in an e-mail interview last month how becoming a mother has changed my poetry. I answered glibly, something about motherhood taking most of my writing time. But the question's been nagging me since. I think now that I should have said becoming a mother freed me, and compelled me, to explore more visceral, physical subject matter, and reminded me how funny the world can be.

Both of those discoveries might not seem particularly revelatory, but they are so, at least a little bit, for someone with my rarefied upbringing on the North Shore of Lake Michigan, about thirty miles from Chicago. As a day student I attended Woodlands Academy of the Sacred Heart, a private Catholic all-girl boarding school. There are some good arguments for single-sex education—for instance, studies have shown that in coed high schools, male students get called on more frequently than females, and teachers are more likely to challenge or prod male students with follow-up questions. Get the females their own classroom, the idea follows, and THEY will be the ones called on; THEY will be asked the follow-up questions, and when the time comes for student governance, they will not only be class secretary but the vice president and president too, and in this way gain confidence and leadership skills, and someday perhaps move from president of the class to president of the country.

But Woodlands was no training ground for nascent feminists. We paid more attention to our developing breasts than our developing sense of self. One would guess that in a single-sex environment, students would be free from the pressure to be physically attractive. To the contrary, I've never been anyplace where beauty mattered more. Not that this was openly acknowledged—body issues, like sex, or anything controversial or unsavory, were simply not discussed. Perhaps that's why so many of the girls seemed messed up. Or perhaps it was because they came from families that were very, very rich, and very, very troubled. Whatever the cause, at Woodlands, you were popular in proportion to your number of eating disorders. If you had bulimia *and* anorexia, well, you were definitely "in." I don't recall a lot of learning going on, little intellectual vigor from the students, little from the teachers. The small amount of poetry we were taught was ladylike and pious. The only poem we studied by Emily Dickinson, for example, was "I'm nobody!/Who are you?/Are you—Nobody—Too?"—without a doubt, Dickinson's only cute poem. Her poems about ambition—"I play at Riches—to appease/The Clamoring for Gold"—or passion—"I see thee better—in the Dark"—well, these were skipped over in our classroom text.

My father would only agree to pay for college if I attended a Catholic school, so because going ROTC held little appeal, I went to the University of Notre Dame, where one would think I'd get more of the same—after all, it's very traditional, patriarchal, and had a high male-to-female student ratio. But it's here that I had my first good teachers who showed me good poetry and how daring it could be.

Slowly I began to grow frustrated with the limitations of "acceptable subject matter" and the poetry of morals. In one poetry workshop, the professor asked students to bring in poems they admired. Someone brought in "Bulimia" by a young poet named Denise Duhamel. The poem described the bulimic's stealthy consumption of a wedding cake she'd ordered at a bakery across town and her subsequent vomiting. After the poem was read, I said nothing, just looked around the circle of students to see if anyone else was stunned. Women weren't supposed to have appetites, much less talk about them so nakedly. The frankness of the sexual metaphors and the almost-prose factualness created a tone that was consciously unpretty ("As ingenious as the first/few times she would consciously masturbate, making note of where/her fingers felt best, she devised a way to vomit/that only hurts a second"). What would they say back at Woodlands? Wasn't this Duhamel person worried about people thinking *she* was the bulimic? Or—even worse—that *she* masturbated?

Eventually, I learned to admire this kind of honesty, and by this point I'd made it to Arkansas and learned to hail the red taxi, but I still wasn't interested in exposing my own life. It just didn't seem interesting enough to me—I was more curious about other people. Several of the poems in my first book are written in the voice of personae, like Mary Milton or Gauguin's daughter. But the process of birthing Claire changed what I wanted to write about. It left me feeling betrayed that I'd been unprepared for the pure animal nature of birth. For the first time, I understood myself to be a mammal with a mammal's instincts and desires beneath the veneer of civilization—a mammal just as much as the opossum with its thirteen nipples. The nakedness I felt needed a naked kind of poetry, because I owned my body in a new way now. I was more consciously physical. I had brushed against my own boundaries, knew my outlines. I knew how far I could stretch before I burst at the seams, because in delivery I had stretched until that point, and then burst at the seams.

A web site called PregnancyDaily.com reports that in a contemporary motherhood study, when women were asked "Is looking after the baby anything like you thought it would be?" only 9 percent said yes. The most common reactions to new motherhood included "shock, being unprepared, panic, anxiety, and feeling out of control." I began to see that many new mothers feel betrayed by all that's been kept from them, and poetry was the tool I used to critique this betrayal. So, in my second book, I had a speaker called "Beth Ann," with a baby named "Claire," a person so deeply involved in what she was going through that she stopped being self-conscious, and stopped writing the poetic equivalent of "Do I look fat in these pants?"

Having Claire also reminded me how much humor exists in everyday situations, even if we get out of the habit of seeing it. I've read that toddlers laugh an average of four hundred times a day, while adults laugh an average of five. I think parents of toddlers split the difference. Being a mommy is tremendously sweet, which we all know; it's also tremendously funny, which isn't so well recognized. Was I the only mother who peed when she coughed the first few weeks? Who felt jealous when her child came home from day care smelling like another woman's perfume? All the unpredictability and absurdity of life with a newborn could move me to laughter as much as to frustration. And

Claire's laughter—even when it was just a fake sneeze that delighted her—could also move me to laughter. Having Claire made me realize that what I like about being a mommy is what I like in a poem—the ability not to take oneself too seriously. I think humor is a strategy earlier women poets didn't feel so free to use. Perhaps, for a long time, women poets had to prove they could handle the big subjects as well as the men and so avoided humor, which would cause them to be dismissed as a poetaster or dabbler in light verse. But now that the generations of women poets before my own (thank you, sisters) have established their seriousness, we're free to establish our playfulness, too, and we can investigate the full range of emotions.

I won't have a chance to amend that interview, dear K, but I've at least been able to come closer to answering the question for my own satisfaction, and to give credit to that thirty-two pound-lion who is right now growling at my closed door. I love that she likes playing lion as well as kitty. My wish for her: that she never fits in at the Woodlands Academies of the world either. Life's too delicious. Here, take a spoon, dig in.

Love,
Beth Ann

June 16, 2004
Dear K,

I'm sure you know the famous panel from the ceiling of the Sistine Chapel, *The Creation of Adam*. I saw it in Rome, where Tommy and I went last summer for our five-year wedding anniversary. We had the most amazing tour guide, Enrico Bruschini, the official art historian of the U.S. Embassy—Enrico has published guides to the Vatican museums—so we arranged in advance to have a tour the day after we arrived.

The night we landed in Rome, we wanted to find a perfect outdoor restaurant with gnocchi and Parmesan and good red wine, but first we needed to collect lire from an ATM. Tommy put our bank card in, but no money came out. And no card was returned. While I don't speak Italian, I have enough Spanish to know that the screen was now flashing "Broken." We punched in our pin number what must have been a hundred times before giving up. There didn't seem to be much we could do except return in the morning before the bank opened and ask an employee to retrieve our card. We both pretended that was likely to happen and continued with our dinner plans, but now we were more like Milton's Adam and Eve after being kicked out of the garden: "They hand in hand with wand'ring steps and slow,/Through Eden took their solitary way."

The next morning I was waiting at the bank when it opened, but there was no bank card inside the machine. So I found a pay phone and called Amex to learn that our account was already maxxed out.

"The first charge," the representative said, "is twenty-five hundred euros for an orange leather jacket."

"But I don't even wear orange, it would clash with my ha-ha-hair," I sobbed into the receiver. She promised to look into the matter.

We needed to call our bank back in Mississippi, but it was Friday, the Fourth of July. That meant the bank was closed and we had to wait until Monday to know whether our account would be reimbursed. We'd learn, when we did get through, that we wouldn't be responsible for any of the charges. Apparently these ATM scams were common in Rome. Thieves put two-sided tape in the machine after hours, then wait for unsuspecting tourists. After the tourist leaves with his card jammed in the machine, they fish the tape, and the card, back out, and go shopping for orange leather jackets. Which is how, dear K, I learned you should never use a bank machine in a foreign country unless the bank is open. But I'm getting ahead of myself—blame it on the double cappuccino I had before beginning this letter. After we had learned that we'd have days to wait until we knew whether we'd be reimbursed, we were to meet Enrico. I was so distracted and upset I didn't think I'd be able to enjoy the art, but I was wrong.

Enrico took us through a little-known entrance so we could beat the crowds to the Sistine Chapel. We stood directly under *The Creation of Adam*, which shows a reclining Adam, nude, propping up a listless elbow on his knee, waiting for God to give him the spark of life. Reaching from the right side, God hovers in front of a group of cherubs, all of them backed by a flowing, curved red mantle. He strains to extend his forefinger to connect with the clay Adam. Enrico asked us, as we were standing beneath the painting, craning our heads up, as hundreds of schoolchildren, gaggles of nuns, and Babels of tour groups filed into the room, what the red mantle looks like. I couldn't discern it at first, and then suddenly, there it was: the mantle was the shape, color, and position of a uterus. Enrico lowered his upraised face to give me a toothy grin and I felt proud as a schoolgirl. Then he pointed out an added detail—below the red mantle, floating free of the figure of God, is a green veil, in the very position of a just-cut umbilical cord.

Many times I have seen, in art or sculpture, representations of God giving life to humanity, but never has it felt as moving as there on the richly restored chapel ceiling, with God's passion for the new creation seen maternally. God portrayed as the mother—it made me think how the delivery might have been painful, traumatic, though beautiful. And finally I understood why Adam is painted with a belly button.

Does this uterus business sound far-fetched? Back in the States, I checked out some books on Michelangelo. Although it was against the law to dissect and study cadavers, Michelangelo broke this law; we know because we have his studies. Trained first as a sculptor, he had thoroughly studied the human form, and wanted to show off what he knew. Also, Michelangelo often embedded symbols in his work. He used his own self-portrait, for example, in the flayed face of St. Bartholomew, who was skinned alive, and he painted a critic he despised as one of the sinners descending into hell—a sinner whose testicles were being gnawed by a snake. Do you have a reproduction of *The Creation of Adam* in any of your art books? Compare it to a transverse diagram of the uterus from *What to Expect When You're Expecting,* and you'll see what I mean.

I want to tell you about the other work of art by Michelangelo that has given me solace, when most religious art puts me in mind of a quip by Erica Jong: "Women are the only exploited group in history who have been idealized into powerlessness."

It's *The Pietà,* which is in a little alcove of St. Peter's Basilica. I had seen its image many times, but not until I was standing in front of it did I understand that it's a very strange sculpture. And it took me a while to discern why. Now I'm not saying it's not skillfully rendered—you'd think you could run your fingers though the Virgin's mantle, though it's carved of Carrara marble. But there's something about it decidedly off-kilter. Or three things, actually.

The first is that the Virgin looks too young. Jesus was supposed to be thirty-three when he was crucified, and the Virgin's face here is completely unlined, like a woman of twenty.

The second strangeness is that she looks composed. Her face is free of tears and rage—yet she's holding in her lap her newly dead son, just released from his torturous death on the Cross. It's true that it was a convention to show Mary's face as calm, but Michelangelo was nothing if not unconventional. A glance at his sinners in the Last Judgment proves that he could paint fear and horror quite realistically.

The third strange thing is that the Virgin is huge compared to Christ. Imagine her standing and you realize she'd tower over him—she's at least three times his size.

Enrico of course had heard these observations before, and had heard many theories from art historians to account for them. He shared with me two salient ones. The first is that Michelangelo lost his mother when he was only six years old, and created in the face and scale of the Virgin the mother he remembers from his boyhood.

The second theory, more convincing to me, is that *The Pietà* represents a vision Mary had when she held the infant Christ on her lap. She understands with a terrible foreknowledge that her son will die in a violent manner, and out of great love and devotion, she bows to God's will. There seems to be some evidence for this interpretation—Enrico pointed out that she cradles Jesus's neck, for example, the same way you cradle a newborn's. Her size, her youth, and her facial expression are more in keeping with a young woman kenning the future than a middle-aged woman holding a dead son. And to think that Mary, just having given birth and filled with love for her newborn, might glimpse his horrific death moved me with an empathy that I'd never felt before any other Pietà, a scene long familiar from my Catholic-school days.

So you can see why I was able to forget, at least for a while, the fear that our account was bulldozed the first day of our ten-day tour of Italy. Forget, at least for a while, how much crime and ugliness skulks through human nature. And I'm grateful to Michelangelo for that. He lifted me to a refined place of color and form, then set me back down in the world, this sordid, magnificent, redeeming world.

Love,
Beth Ann

June 22, 2004
Dear K,

Oh, people told me that same thing—you won't remember the pain. *You won't remember the pain, you won't remember the pain.* And do I remember the pain? No, I think, somehow, and also yes. Yes, and also, somehow, no. Sorry to equivocate, my dear; I'd like to straighten this out myself.

Let's see: If women agree that giving birth is the most intense physical experience possible, and we do, we also must admit it seems strangely flattened out in memory, as if an iceberg has slid over it, sloughing the rocky summits and valleys of the contractions to gently rounded hills. And I'm a good test case, as I had natural childbirth so I can't blame memory loss on pain medication. Well, what accounts for the flattening?

An answer comes from an unlikely source: scientists researching marijuana. It turns out that a woman going through labor has a natural way of producing a chemical compound similar to marijuana. I read about this in a fascinating book called *The Botany of Desire: A Plant's-Eye View of the World*, by Michael Pollan. In one section of the book, Pollan looks at marijuana research. The active ingredient of the plant, THC, was identified in the mid-sixties. Next, scientists sought to trace what THC does after entering the brain. In 1988, the nerve cells that THC binds to, called "cannabinoid receptors," were discovered. Just as a key fits a lock, THC fits these receptors, and that unlocking results in the cognitive changes we call "getting stoned." Yet it didn't make sense that our brains would have evolved receptors precisely adapted to the leaves of a plant that, who knows, no one may ever have decided to smoke. This led researchers to the hypothesis that the brain must make its own chemical similar to THC, which would unlock the same receptors in the brain. This hypothesis turned out to be true—in 1992, researchers discovered that the brain makes its own "endogenous cannabinoid."

This discovery has scientists asking the question—why would the body *want* to replicate the effects of marijuana, effects which include pain reduction, sedating of the emotions, short-term memory loss, and minor cognitive impairment? What possible evolutionary benefit could the body derive? A key lies in where some of these cannabinoid receptors have been found. In addition to being located in the brain, they've been discovered in the uterus. This means that the uterus has receptors that, when triggered by a cannabinoid neurotransmitter, pretty much take a big bong hit. The result is that, first, the pain of childbirth is dulled; then, later, the brain forgets precisely how much the body agonized. Hence the evolutionary advantage: if we could remember how much the first birth hurt, we'd never have a second child. Pretty trippy stuff.

So that's the scientist's response, and to that I'll add the poet's response. I think our inability to recall and relive the memory of the pain has to do with the fact that during hard labor, you go to a place beyond language. It isn't so much that there are no good words to describe what you're going through as that there are *no* words. You're a white wave in a white sea, without boundaries or cognition. Margaret Atwood captures this beautifully in her short story "Giving Birth." Atwood's narrator is advised to take an epidural so she doesn't have to go through pain. She thinks, *What pain?* . . . When there is no pain she feels nothing, when there is pain, she feels nothing because there is no she." We use the word "disembodied" a lot, but truly it applies here because the body breaks free from the ego. It's believed that children's language acquisition is tied to their ability to make memories, that only when they can name things can they store them in their memories and recall them later. If this is true, it follows that the word-lessness of giving birth makes it more abstract and therefore less easily recalled.

When I try, really try, to place myself back in the delivery room, I see myself from above, as if the me I am now watches the old me from the ceiling, like an angel, or a video camera on a dolly. And the details I remember are the same ones I put in the poem I wrote about giving birth—the first poem in *Tender Hooks*, "Bite Me." And a lot of those details aren't even from the delivery itself but are things I noticed in the days after the delivery—that the whites of my eyes were bright red from burst blood vessels, that my chest and neck were bruised from the exertion of the pushing stage, that I looked like I'd been in the ring with a boxer and lost badly, I was so blue-green and swollen. There's only one detail in the poem that came from the delivery itself, after Claire got stuck in the birth canal with her arms crossed behind her head, and I had to push her shoulders and elbows out at the same time that I pushed her head out—that "my asshole turned inside out like a rosebud." And this is a detail Tommy told me about later, as he was down at the foot of the cot with the midwife, poor guy, a blood-splattered soldier on the front line.

Of course the very act of writing changes memory—it wires together certain neurons in neon merely because they are written down, and because they are written down, they become both fixed and false, because no act can ever be truly and completely represented by words—every experience is clarified, codified, condensed. Before memories are written down, they are organic, can shift and swirl, and details may be highlighted now that may be shaded during the next recollection. But once a memory is pinned down on paper, it is as lifeless as a butterfly pinned down on paper. More useful, more beautiful, perhaps, but no longer alive.

And here's a third reason that could account for the amnesia: the pain is overshadowed and overwhelmed by the wordless joy of holding the baby, at last. It's not that we forget the pain so much as that when we give birth, we too are reborn, and we recollect the pain as belonging to the old life, the way the butterfly unfolding her wet wings recollects the cocoon.

Love,
Beth Ann

June 24, 2004
Dear One—

This morning, watching some cartoons with Claire, I saw her pull her T-shirt up over her potbelly and tuck the end under. "What are you doing, sweetie?" I asked, and she said, "I want a short shirt." I realized she meant a midriff-baring top like those worn by the girls dancing in praise of the Gap—and I felt horrified that at age three she recognizes and desires their sex appeal.

Mostly when I see Claire make developmental or cognitive leaps, I'm delighted. I think of bending over her crib and watching her turn over for the first time and letting out a whoop—later a Jewish friend gave me a great word for what I'd done. I'd been *kvelling*: "to exclaim joyfully or proudly, especially in boasting about the achievements of a family member." But not all parts of her growing up bring me unmitigated joy. I remember the first time I felt this way: Claire was probably sixteen months, and I was bathing her, which she's always hated. (No wonder the swim lessons were a bust.) The part she hated most was when I'd rinse the shampoo out of her hair. To help her through, I established a little ritual where, as I poured the warm water down her head, I'd croon, "Almost done . . . almost done . . . almost done," and on the last rinse I'd say, "All better," and she'd chime in to say it with me.

Well, one time I was bathing her and was very distracted—I was talking to Tommy about how we'd work out the day's scheduling because we both needed the car, and in the background someone was leaving a message on the answering machine because we hadn't picked up the phone. Claire said "All better," so I took her out of the tub and was toweling her off when I realized her hair wasn't wet. Isn't that funny, I thought—she made a mistake. But then I had a strange, new maternal instinct. I swiveled her little toweled shoulders around so I could look into her eyes, and when I did I saw an evil gleam in them. My daughter had told her first lie. For a second, I even felt oddly proud; surely other children aren't lying until they're two at least—my daughter's gifted!

Anyway, after the short-shirt episode, it was time to turn the TV off. I pulled out Milne's *The House at Pooh Corner* instead, and found a bit of grown-up wisdom in it: "Poetry and Hums aren't things which you get, they're things which get *you*. And all you can do is to go where they can find you."

Please excuse the brevity of this letter; my desk is calling. Some days, the lucky days, that's where poetry can find me.

Your pal,
Beth Ann

June 29, 2004

Another thing I love about parenthood, dear K—it ushers in a return to the magic of music.

There's not a day that goes by now in which I don't sing—and there hasn't been since I started singing to my big ole belly, my Claire-in-there, as we called her.

Prior to these four years, when did I sing? Church, sometimes, when I went—sometimes not even then. Christmas carols, maybe. In the car, if no one could see me or hear me. And I love to sing! I think nearly everyone does, though some of us have been shamed out of it by being told that our voices are poor. Now that I think about it, perhaps there are only two occasions when Americans sing: "The Star-Spangled Banner" at baseball games, and the predictably tedious "Happy Birthday" at parties. But there's something about feeling that column of air rise up our windpipe that connects us to our most basic physical pleasure. We are rhythmical animals, from our heartbeats to our cycles of eating and sleeping, and when we create rhythms, we're in harmony with our bodies.

We sing so infrequently now, we hardly know any lyrics. America has virtually no tradition of folk songs—something I realized during the year I spent in the Czech Republic, where the two questions that never failed to amaze me were "What languages do you speak?" and "What instruments do you play?" The Czechs, you see, all knew three or four of each. They could sing folk songs for hours, naturally assuming harmonies. On camping trips, around a fire, the guitar would pass from hand to hand—everyone could take a turn. When I received the guitar and turned to pass it to my neighbor, they protested—they thought I must be so good that I didn't want to show them up!

How different our culture, in which we don't even sing on long road trips anymore because each family member has a Walkman.

And so the mechanical, perfect percussion laid down by the drum machine replaces the imperfectly clapping hands and the tapping feet. I read that there even are health benefits to drumming. According to the Fall/Winter 2003 issue of *Advances in Mind-Body Medicine*, seniors who thought they were taking part in a drumming class—really a study—reported feeling less anger and depression and more energy during the six-week session. Yet drumming, with the exception of Native American religious ceremonies, is left out of daily life. Oh, I hate the tone I'm taking, the grouchy arrogance of the old, gloating that the world is going downhill. But I do feel that some essential part of human nature needs to pound percussion on a table ledge, or belt out "There's No Business Like Show Business" every now and again.

When Baby comes, we remember this. Baby comes, and Baby is furious. Those books which say that babies don't have emotions until they are older? Burn them. Dance on the ashes. Baby can work herself up into such a dervish of screaming emotion that her whole body vibrates. Baby squinches herself into a fist. Baby is inconsolable. No words, no car trip, no buckin' bronco ride on the clothes dryer soothes Baby. Then Mother rocks Baby and finds a hum low in her chest that cleats its way up her rusty throat. And Baby is still angry, but less so. More seconds fill the spaces between sobs. Mother hums louder, soon whole words are tumbling from her mothertongue rough as a cat's, and inconsolable Baby is consoled, the fiddlehead ferns of Baby's fingers uncurl, the shuddering breath smooths itself, the eyes are slate-blue slits and then smaller slits and then only slivers of white as Baby's eyes roll back and Baby's sleeping, mouth open with the sweet milk breath Mother would like to bottle and wear as eau de cologne when Baby is grown and gone, Baby is dreaming and Mother's music is the lily pad on which Baby is the floating, and Mother is still humming although she could stop now, but now it is for herself she hums, it is her swan song for her cygnet and her infant self, she is crooning the way she was crooned to, a song she knows by heart, a song she would have sworn she had forgotten.

Love,
Beth Ann

July 2, 2004
Dear One,

This morning after breakfast (for Claire, the strawberries she picked out of my bowl of Special K with Strawberries; for me, the leftover flakes) I was pushing Claire on the swing and thought, like a kick in the gut, that there will never be another summer in which she is three years old. Never another summer during which I place my hands low on her three-year-old back and propel her pointed toes toward the sky, sky which she thinks she can toe if she swings high enough. Never another summer with her small, firm, warm, ordinary, miraculous three-year-old back.

Push—one-time-only . . .
Push—limited engagement . . .
Push—everything must go . . .

Love,
BA

July 5, 2004
Dear K,

Today I sit down to write you and think, Who am I to advise? Feeling frustrated with myself after a few unpleasant run-ins for which I'm to blame. I had a quick lunch with Ann today, newly back from Sweden and Paris, and I could feel her being reserved with me, wasn't sure if it was just jet lag. Finally she worked up to tell me that her feelings were hurt that I didn't invite her to Tommy's birthday party on Saturday. She wondered—Did I think she was too old? Which is crazy, of course, I love her, admire her.

I've seen her twice since she's been home, but both times I was rushed, and I just plain forgot to tell her about the party. But even as I explained this to her I felt awkward, dissembling. "Oh, Ann, we've invited all kinds of people to this party," I told her. And then I felt twice as wretched, as if saying, Look, we're inviting lots of old people.

I've got to learn to slow down. I sprint through my days, sacrificing what I can. I don't blow-dry my hair anymore. I don't try on clothes—I just buy what I need and return what doesn't work. When I throw a dinner party, I accept guests' offers to bring appetizers. And salads. But there still isn't enough time to do all I need. I don't want to be one of those women who never volunteers as room mother, who brings cookies to the school bake sale in a bakery box. Nor do I want my answer to "Did you see this week's *New Yorker?*" to always be "No." Nor do I want to give up my friendships and pen pals. Basically, I want it all.

But I feel so . . . precipitous, skittery. The last time my mother was here, I broke a ceramic planter by banging it against the faucet when I was watering it. "I'm so clumsy," I said with a sigh. "No, Beth Ann, you're not clumsy," she said. "You just move too quickly." And she of course is right.

Oh K, no advice today, I'm afraid, unless you can spare some for your old friend,

Beth Ann

July 12, 2004
Dear One,

What a stupid day I've had. I leave tomorrow for the Sewanee
Writers' Conference and won't return until July 25. I knew today
would involve errands, but I'd planned to start the day writing
you a letter (last night, I'd grown happy at the thought: sitting in
the big chair by the picture window with a mug of coffee, scribbling, perhaps taking a break to water the flowers, leaving sips of
water in the tiny purple cornucopias of my birthday butterfly
bush for the long tongues of the butterflies which have come at
last and rise and fall and rise and fall on their papery hinges).

But instead of letter writing I was chasing down the contractor, who eventually came to talk about the roof, and the morning
was chipped off into shards of follow-up phone calls and check-
book tallying. Oh K, it's so hot here, mosquitoes big as basset
hounds, every afternoon dumps a platter of rain. It's so damn
humid, mushrooms popping up like periscopes, everything
steamy, sweaty, beaded, the glass of sweet tea fogging with your
breath as you sip, sunglasses fogging as you bend into the car,
the shower tiles caulked with mildew, the wet clothing in the

washer musty if ignored for even a few hours. And finally this: mold on our ceiling, black-speckled swirls moving from the out-side edges in like a swarm of gnats, and the paint peeling off in ripped tongues. But it needs more than a simple sanding and repainting, says the contractor, whom I take at his word because I have no other word to take. No, the roof must have a venting ridge so the hot air can escape. And there goes two thousand dol-lars. Which probably means three thousand dollars, and now I regret turning down summer teaching . . .

I suppose I could look on the bright side and say at least while the work is being done we'll all be in Sewanee so Claire won't inhale the fumes, but right this minute I'm disinclined to find the bright side.

Dear K, write me a letter about the weather in Alaska. Tuck a sea breeze in the envelope, and post it right away.

Love,
Beth Ann

July 15, 2004
Hello from Sewanee, TN, dear one—

It's lovely to be back at the University of the South for these twelve days. Tommy and I first came to this conference in '99, when he had a fellowship to attend and I had a scholarship (you need a published book to be a fellow, and I hadn't finished *Open House* yet). Now we've been lucky enough to land another visit here—this time I'm a fellow, and he's my cabana boy. For the middle few days of the conference my mom will take Claire to her home in Chicago. So I'll get both family time and selfish-poet-playtime.

This morning, I got up early and walked to breakfast by myself to read today's poems for class. I had almost reached the dining hall when I spotted on the side of the curb an enormous moth, size of my palm, with a torso fat and furry and striped yellow and orange like a goldfish. Its wings were eggshell white and brittle-looking in the strong mountain sun, the ends ragged and fluttery ("moth-eaten," one would say, if describing something besides a moth). The bedraggled gown of a runaway bride. And I wished I could have a magical ball gown of a thousand of these moths created by a fairy tailor that would dissolve when I return home at midnight, the thousand moths flying up as one into the night sky.

While I was squatting there, watching the moth, other folks from the conference were walking into the dining hall. But I didn't worry about looking odd, and that's one thing I love about being with writers: we're all so odd that acting odd *is* normal. For example, the sign on the door where a cook had written "todays menu" bothered me, as I'm always bothered when apostrophes go missing—and then I'm bothered that I'm bothered. Breakfast, lunch, and dinner I have suppressed my geeky impulse to correct the sign. But last night I saw that someone less suppressed had penciled in the apostrophe. My lasagna tasted even better as a result. What a bunch of weirdos, always walking around with feathers, dried cicada shells, bones of small animals found in a forest: my people.

So the writing conference folk filed past me as I moved my face slowly closer to the furry creature, though I needn't have worried about it flying away, for it was completely still. It didn't even shutter the eyespots on its wings, the way moths do to scare off predators. Another writer saw what I saw looking at and squatted down beside me. We spoke in whispers as if at a bedside vigil, and perhaps the moth was dying, clinging to the concrete, creature of the night burnt by the Tennessee sun.

Eventually we pushed ourselves to our feet and went in to breakfast. I decided on the way out I would find the moth, and if it was dead, wrap it in a napkin to take to my artist friend Blair who is working on a moth series. But when I finished eating and walked out, I found the moth flattened by a car tire. And felt the wings of melancholy flutter against the cage of my heart.

At dusk when everyone else has left Lake Cheston I think I'll go for a swim and watch the bats loop and skim the surface, gulping down mosquitoes and chasing each dry swallow with a sip of mountain water.

If I can find out the name of the moth, I'll let you know.

Love,
Beth Ann

July 18, 2004
Dear One,

I went to the bookstore to look up the moth in an insect book, but confess that I'm stymied. Emperor moth, saturnid moth, io moth, silkworm moth—no, no, no, and no. I'll keep looking.

After the bookstore, I was sitting outside on a bench when a fiction fellow named Ian squatted down beside me. He'd just finished reading *Tender Hooks*, he said, and then asked, "You had a miscarriage?" It startled me a bit, but now that I've written poems about the miscarriage, most people guess that it's something that happened to me. And the people who ask me about those poems are often people who've had a miscarriage, too.

Ian described his wife's delivery of a stillborn child, midway through her pregnancy. He told me how shocked they were, because everything had been rolling along, nursery painted, mobile hung above the bassinet. But the baby came so early; she was simply too small to live. At the hospital, the doctor said, "Should we take care of it?" meaning, should they cremate the baby. Ian and his wife were numb with shock. Ian nodded dumbly, not even sure what he was agreeing to.

But a few days later, having thawed a bit at the edges, Ian went back to the hospital to claim the ashes. The doctor stammered that he was sorry, but there were no ashes. "Our bodies are mostly water," he told Ian, "and sometimes with a body this small, it simply . . . evaporates." So Ian could only explain to his wife that they had no proof that their daughter Lucy had existed. No ashes to bury, no grave to mark in the family plot, no ceremony through which a spiritual guide could help them grieve and heal.

I told Ian then about the image I can't shake—about leaning against an orderly's arm, being walked to the cot for the D&C, and through the haze of anesthesia seeing a squat metal garbage can beneath the stirrups where my legs would go. The kind of can you'd open with your foot.

Ian and I spoke for a while about our culture's need for a ceremony for the miscarried, and the aborted. Ian's novel deals in part with the death of his daughter, and I asked him if writing about her was a way of creating such a ceremony. For I've felt that writing about my miscarriage provided a kind of marker, proof that the child existed. The white sheet of paper became a kind of gravestone.

It was late then, and because I'd planned to take a swim, I

invited Ian to join me. We walked to Lake Cheston and were the only two there. We shucked off our top layer of clothing and then stood in our bathing suits among the reeds and grasses at the lake edge, and I felt awkward because I imagined what a third party, someone else from the conference, would make of us here alone together, nearly naked, on the darkening water. And I also felt awkward because we'd just met and in such a short time shared so many intimacies; I wasn't sure where our talk could go next. As it happened, we didn't need to talk. We walked slowly into the lake. We let that body of water take us, carry us, we floated separately, companionably, cleansed for a while, and part of something bigger than either of us.

Love,
Beth Ann

July 21, 2004
Hello dear Kathleen—

My mom and Claire left the conference yesterday for their trip to Chicago. I'm so lucky that my mom wants to take Claire and is so good with her. The arrangement is perfect—I couldn't leave

Claire for twelve days, so it was great to have them both here, but I miss out on a lot when I'm in Mom mode. Even when I'm at a lecture and I know Claire is with my mom at the playground, I still can't settle down and be fully attentive—some part of me listens for her cry, jumps at the ring of someone's cell phone. So it was with both relief and regret that I waved goodbye to them as they drove away, Claire's tiny hand flapping above her giant car seat. All afternoon I've felt strangely unmoored. What helped: the cocktail party at the French house, where the writers hang out after the readings. I didn't realize how many gin and tonics I'd had until I stood at the bar for a refill and counted three limes anchoring the bottom of my cup.

I've been thinking today about your letter that arrived the day we left, in which you ask if I think you could handle starting a Ph.D. program with a newborn. I wanted to dash off a reply before we headed out, but now I'm glad I didn't, for my quick response would have been "Of course!" but my more considered response will probably serve you better.

As Tommy drove though the Tennessee countryside and I gazed at the Queen Anne's lace and orange cosmos lining the highways, I considered the things that will help you negotiate the tricky work/family balance. I wouldn't say every woman needs all of the things on my list, but the more you have, the better your chances. Ideally, every woman who hopes to raise children while producing creative work would have: a supportive spouse and extended family, a room of one's own (or at least a corner of a room with a door you can shut), mom friends, writer friends, and mentors.

There are two other things that help. One is to gamble on yourself as an investment that will pay off. It isn't always easy to have this kind of confidence. Sometimes when Claire was very young I'd hire a babysitter to come to the house so I could write. Then I'd be at my desk thinking, Is this poem worth $6.50 an hour? At that thought, whatever little seedling poem I was trying to trellis would shrivel and die. Women aren't normally encouraged to provide themselves time and resources, especially if doing so requires sacrifices from others. But it's a skill we need to practice. So start by faking a confidence in your talents, and after a while you might have the results to justify the confidence.

The second thing I want to pass on is a piece of advice I need to take myself, which is this: Accept mediocrity. Be underwhelming. You can't do everything, so choose some things to sacrifice, and absolve yourself from guilt. It may be that you can raise a child and write a dissertation—but have the ugliest lawn on the block. And that's okay. Let someone else win "Lawn of the Month"—someone with a nanny.

Your pal,
Beth Ann

July 24, 2004
Dear One,

It's my last day at Sewanee, and I'm penning this in paradise, Bridal Veil Falls. After twelve days of being constantly around other people, I wanted to be alone, strain my ears to catch a bit of my own silence. I gave myself, it seems, a time-out.

How intensely green it is here. The very hot, very white July sun is pearled and cooled as it sifts through the various canopies of leaves. Here and there—like white gold that has remained in the prospector's sieve—it spotlights a jack-in-the-pulpit or island of sphagnum moss.

When I'm alone in nature as I am now, I marvel that I ever let a day go by when I'm not alone in nature as I am now. But the truth is, not only days but whole months go by between immersions. How can that be, when I feel so recharged here? I'm sitting on a large flat rock facing the falls, which does indeed look like a bridal veil, as the shallow mountain stream over the years has channeled through the layers of shale and froths as it bounces from ledge to ledge, a lacy mist that falls to the rocks below, about thirty steep feet. Of course, that watery music made me need to pee so I snuck behind a rock, though I probably needn't have been so cautious, as I'm really quite wonderfully alone.

There is not a mother on earth, I bet, who doesn't wish to raise her child differently from her own upbringing in at least one way. I'd like Claire to have a close relationship to the natural world. Having grown up in a prosperous suburb of Chicago, I was shockingly ignorant of nature. Although I spent my endless summers in neighborhood backyards, everything was so ChemLawnesque. Wildlife meant squirrels, robins, mosquitoes, the occasional deer. Bug zappers on every patio spitting their spiteful buzz back to the subdivisioned sky. Say we did spot a turtle, or a snakeskin, or a long striped feather—these were *things not to touch, they give you germs, Beth Ann, go wash your hands.*

Sometimes I think we look in a mirror only once at, say, age eleven, and never really look again. What I mean is, although we continue to grow, our self-image never changes. And the me I saw then wasn't good at sports and wasn't an outdoor kid. I still think of myself as unathletic—but I'm an aerobics instructor! And I think I'm not a nature person, but here I am, meditating about the plants I can see from here, and saying their names aloud for the pleasure of pronouncing—the pinecone mushroom, also called "Old Man of the Woods" because it looks so thorny and grows alone; the white cushion moss, also called "mother-in-law moss," because while it appears to be a comfortable resting place, it traps a surprising amount of water, so inviting your mother-in-law to sit on it means she'll shortly decide to head back home. I can also see a mountain laurel, which manufactures a poisonous honey—I'm told beekeepers can tell when their bees have visited this tree, and they have to keep those bees from reentering the hive—a sip of that honey could kill you.

Thinking about Claire's future relationship to nature also makes me nervous because I have to consider how many of my beloved spots will be gone by the time she's old enough to find them. K, I know I should be doing more to save these places. As a child I read about the civil rights movement and wished I had been alive then because it would have been easy to be heroic; of course I would have ridden with the freedom fighters and marched to Selma. But really it's the passage of time that makes the right side so obviously right and easy. I imagine future generations will fault us for not fighting the destruction of the environment more urgently. I mean sure, Tommy and I recycle, shop at the farmers' market, avoid Wal-Mart, but if, in years to come, Claire asks us what we did to keep the forests from being plundered, will our small concessions be all I have to offer her?

Sweet pal, I have three reasons I must stop this letter. One is, as you probably guessed as my handwriting grows humpbacked, I'm out of paper. Two, the mosquitoes have found me, and they're telling their friends. Three—tomorrow I go home to Tommy and Claire, and I need to pack. Two friends are reading poetry this afternoon, and then there's a dance! I'll wear an apple-green dress that my mother wore in the early seventies with a curvy zipper and bright beachy words—Sand! Surf!—splashed across it. When

Claire was born, we got out my baby photos to compare Claire's infant face to my own. And there was my mother in this dress, holding me on her hip. "Mom, I adore that dress," I said, and she seemed amused—"Well, it's probably still up in the attic . . ." In a minute I'd gotten the flashlight and was pulling down the attic stairs. Oh, that's another thing my mother did right—she kept *everything*. Not me. I travel light, for which Claire will undoubtedly fault me.

Off to put on my dancing shoes,

BA

July 25, 2004
Dear One,

The great nature writers say that to really understand a place one must not leave it, but marry it and study it ceaselessly, intimately, paying attention to its cycles and harmonies. They might be right, but for me travel is a bright kaleidoscope that returns me home with freshly shaken eyes, ready to see. In these twelve days I've been away the crepe myrtles have bloomed, and as my pal David dropped me off they shook their fuchsia maracas at me so I would admire them.

Rats, but Claire has already gone down for her nap—I'd hoped to arrive home earlier. I hungered to see Claire before she slept, to stick my nose into the crevice where her neck meets her chin, that tent of flesh that, when she was an infant, could collect little sticky beads or smell slightly yogurty from spit-up. Instead, I merely gazed at her as she napped. Three days since I've held her and already she looks bigger.

Tommy rubbed my feet while I looked over my mail. Three delicious letters from you, dear pal—what a richness among the bills and catalogues, all the detritus of acquisition, to hear your sweetscratchy voice.

I'd like to copy out a quote from Goethe, as a kind of thanks: "The world is so empty if one thinks only of mountains, rivers, and cities; but to know someone who thinks and feels with us, and who, though distant, is close to us in spirit, this makes the earth for us an inhabited garden."

I'll write more tomorrow. I can't help myself, I'm going to go wake up my Claire Bear.

Love,
BA

July 26, 2004
Dear Kathleen,

Claire's been really clingy this morning, which is natural after three days apart, but the house is a wreck and I can't even see the blue basket beneath the mountain of dirty laundry, and she insists on watching Teletubbies from the pretzel of my folded legs. I started to read a letter behind her back, and when she caught me she said, "Mommy, you're not looking at me," and began to cry. I felt like a horse dying to buck her rider. Days like this put the *s* before the word "motherhood."

I suppose I'm chafing this morning because the unreal days in Sewanee were like a crystallization of my previous life. After Tommy and Claire left, I regressed back to the old BA, someone less encumbered, more selfish, more fun—someone I miss. I stayed up till three talking poetry and drinking with new writer pals who'd lived on fishing boats in Alaska or ashrams in India, then I wandered to the porch where others were telling jokes or playing guitar. And there was so much sexual tension. With twelve days away from spouses and families in this Disneyland of fun and intellectual stimulation, everyone's hormones battered around the room like sparrows trapped in a chimney. Usually at parties I have not only Tommy as my date but Claire on my hip, and while I love that, it was so nice to feel almost-pretend single, to remember other uses for the hips, to unfold a bit in the male gaze like early daffodils giving themselves over to the warm breath of spring.

Of course, there was an alarming aspect to all of the hormones flying around; I saw a few couples slinking off from the final party into the honeysuckle hedges—people with spouses at home. Even I realized it was time to remove myself from temptation— the last night after dinner a bunch of us all piled in a Jeep and drove to the lookout over Shakerag Hollow. It was dusky and a bit foggy as if someone had poured bluing into the washer, and really beautiful. I think we all felt pensive knowing that we'd become close and yet most of us wouldn't see each other again. On the drive home, sitting next to me in the crowded Jeep, was a poet with whom I'd flirted outrageously all week, just for fun. But thigh-to-thigh on the bumpy road, with his arm resting along the back of the seat, brushing my shoulder, I felt I had placed myself in danger, and the gentle friction might cause me to burst into flames. When the car stopped, I wanted to stay where I was, so I sprinted into the party.

Of course I'm glad to be home, but this is a part of motherhood that you might as well know about: while it's important to keep developing the parts of you that you enjoyed before you were a mom, it can be wrenching to have to shift back into Mom-mode so thoroughly. And wrench you must, for there's zero transition time, not even a phone booth to change in. The child doesn't know you've been masquerading as the old BA. The child would rank the possibility of the old BA's existence as less certain than the Easter Bunny. So girl, get used to it: one minute you're at a party in your red cowboy hat discussing Milton's syntax in *Paradise Lost* while someone named Ryder refreshes your cocktail; the next minute you are watching the same Scooby-Doo trotting past the same portrait-with-roving-eyes that you've already seen twice this morning, and your biggest triumph comes from catching your daughter's index finger just before it reaches her mouth, thus depriving her of a booger Scooby Snack.

Love,
BA

July 27, 2004
Dear One—

Oh I'm ashamed of my last letter to you, disgusting self-pity, conceit. Ugh, if the mail were still in the box I'd steal it back. But I suppose it's better that I can't. "Warts and all," as we agreed . . .

Listen, all that appetite, the ambition and ego, that's the worst part of me. Luckily, I know that, most of the time. Hanging out at a writers' conference isn't being a writer. It's the *reward* for being a writer.

As for the other stupid desires I mentioned in my letter—well, it's true I sometimes feel nostalgic for being single, but there's a quick cure for that: spending an evening in the singles bars with my single friends.

I know both marriage and parenthood have made me a better person, less self-involved, more generous, more empathetic. I wouldn't trade the richness that comes from these continually deepening relationships. Sure, feeling almost-single is sexy, but I know that for Tommy and me, marriage is truly the sexiest thing. For us—this is something people don't talk about, I guess—the sex keeps getting better. I'm freer in our married sex life, don't feel shame or self-consciousness about expressing fantasies or taking charge, don't worry if my ass looks big, don't worry if I'm hogging all the pleasure one night because life is long and strange and we have more nights and days in which to meet and mate and make our creaky mattress limp toward song—everything is infinite-seeming, the curve of his penis like the curve of our good earth.

My God, when I think of him bending over my face in the delivery room—he was spooning me ice chips because it was all he knew to do, and when I could I accepted them even though I needed all my concentration for tearing open my body to get that baby out, he was at my feet with the midwife, then back at my face with the spoon of ice chips, jittery like a mosquito bumping around my head, but when there was a break in the contractions I turned to him and he looked back at me through his glasses that were flecked with blood, my blood, and the eyes behind them were cracked with terror and I knew things weren't going well and I knew too that if I died he would die and I knew too that this was our blood oath, we were bound for life.

Love,
Beth Ann

July 28, 2004
Dear K,

Was thinking this morning that, after a few days apart, Claire and I have to reconnect in a way that's very physical and animalistic, much more so than the way she reconnects with Tommy. Almost immediately after waking up this morning, before I'd had my coffee even, she said, "Mommy, let's roll on the floor," so we did. I cradled her along the length of my body, with one arm behind her head, and I held her against me and rolled over and over on the carpet until we were both giggling and dizzy and studded with fuzz, and even then she shrieked, "More, Mommy, more."

I love this rough-and-tumble because it's one way to touch her; I'm very affectionate and wish she were more so. She's never been a big snuggler, and what snuggling she does, she does with Tommy. This has been one of the hardest things I've had to deal with—she prefers his lap for watching movies, prefers his hand to hold while crossing the street. It's made me jealous in the past. Oh, why pretend to be mature: it makes me jealous now! This is why, if we're able to make a second baby, I want a boy—someone to like me better! Someone to even out the odds!

Deep down, I know she's had to distance herself from me a bit in order to establish her emerging selfhood. I've read that for a while infants don't understand they are separate beings from the mother. And of course, before that, she wasn't separate—she was tethered to me like a dinghy to a pier. So—and feel free to call me on this if you think I'm just rationalizing—I think part of her preference for Tommy is aligning herself with He-Who-Is-Not-Mommy, as part of the natural urge for independence.

While it's true she's more affectionate with Tommy, it's also true that my body is the core of her physical relationships—her touchstone. She is no longer tethered to me from the inside, but the connection, while more attenuated, still exists. Often today she touched my breasts. I remember noticing this habit a few months after I'd weaned her. Although she seems to have no memory of being breast-fed, sometimes when she's feeling uncomfortable—say, at a party where every face is strange—as she straddles my hip while I greet my friends, she fiddles with the strap of my tank top or even lightly runs her fingers over the outside of my sweater. I know, at the deepest level, that my body is where she returns when the world threatens her.

My old roomie Carmen has a similar dynamic with her oldest daughter, Isabella. Carmen has a prominent birthmark on her chest, and when Isabella was breast-feeding, she used to rub it lightly as she suckled. Probably she was drawn to it because babies see in black and white until they're six months old, and so the mark must have stood out against Carmen's skin while also providing a bit of texture. Much later, when I was visiting Carmen, Isabella fell off her swing and began crying. Carmen picked her up and hugged her, and I saw Isabella's fingers unconsciously spider down from Carmen's neck to rub the birthmark.

Love,
Beth Ann

August 1, 2004
Dear K,

Today, in the gym's locker room, I heard a woman exclaim to her friend, "God, I just hate kids. And I hate people with kids." I hid behind the plastic shower curtain until I heard their locker doors slam and their voices grow distant, then I gathered my things and slunk away.

Later I figured they were probably reacting to fees being raised to extend day-care hours. But before I figured that out, I started thinking about how poorly childless women are sometimes treated. Because I was thirty before I had Claire, I got occasional doses of the bland arrogance, the if-you-ain't-got-kids-you-ain't-got-nothing types, women who seemed to speak in code to other mothers, who look down on childless women. Once at a baby shower when I was handing my gift to the mother-to-be, my fingernail snapped off.

"Rats," I announced to the room full of mothers, "I broke a nail."

"I remember when I cared about stuff like that," said one mother, and the room broke up in laughter. I chuckled along but understood that my life seemed trivial to these women who were trading the names of babysitters like stock tips. The other day, a student who's thirty-three said that she hates to go home for Thanksgiving because she *still* has to sit at the kids' table. If she doesn't have a child, she must be one. Let's swear, dear K, never to treat childless women this way.

I've also discovered, now that I have a child, that some people find babies creepy. Well, why not? Think of babies emerging, cone-headed, clogged with phlegm, waxy or flaky or webbed with bloody strings. Blue veins marbling the skin. Or bronzed with jaundice. Or crannied with vernix like cream cheese in a bagel. Or molting like a snake. Even wiped down, those early days, they are blind and shaky, something turtlelike about the wrinkled neck and the giant tomato head that lolls and nods, too heavy for its stalk. Something froggish about a newborn on his back, splay-legged, the belly that's wider than the chest.

When Claire was an infant and being cooed over, a young woman might turn to her boyfriend and say, "Bruce, you've gotta hold this baby, she's so sweet," and Bruce would find something crucial to do with his hands instead, like rattle pocket change. And then one day Bruce becomes a daddy, and as he pushes his puffy wife in the hospital wheelchair to the car, she's cooing to the bundle in her arms and he's thinking he'd like to give them both a big shove and take off in the Mustang to Vegas. But instead Bruce buckles the kid into the new car seat and drives them home where there's no instruction manual, the child can't even protect himself from himself, spastic fists the size of walnuts boxing an ear, or a bendy fingernail scratching a seam of blood across a pimpled cheek. Those fists will grasp any finger placed inside them, no matter whose, so many bad people out there, so many bad fingers. Oh the poor, newly vulnerable Bruces.

Even Tommy had moments during my pregnancy when he didn't want to be a father. For me, it was love at first thought, but poor sweet Tommy who catches snakes, even poisonous ones, knows their names and habits and markings—Tommy held her that first day (her foot soles still black from the ink pad, so freshly minted, this treasure) as though she were a hand grenade with the pin pulled.

I have always loved girlie spa things like pedicures and massages, but I've been too poor, or too practical, to have them often. But after the baby came, Tommy gave me gift certificates for the day spa in our town. When Claire was two weeks old, I decided to go in for the massage, partially because Tommy was fretting that I didn't like his gift. It would be the first time I'd been out of the house since returning from the hospital, aside from forays onto our porch to show Claire the sunshine or let her see the house finches who'd built a nest in the wreath on our door. Well, it seemed time; I was finally done with the diapers you wear home from the hospital, done with the sitz bath and the toilet ring and wiping with the medicated pads. And while my body was still pretty torn up, I felt I could climb on the massage table without ripping something open. And I knew it would feel good. My back was still sore from the delivery—at one point when Claire was stuck, I tried squatting, pulling against the bed rails for leverage, and even two weeks later my shoulders ached when I tried to brush my hair. Which wasn't often.

I timed my departure for the spa carefully because the massage was scheduled for an hour and Claire was breast-feeding every hour and a half. Even so, I had to cut the massage short. The masseuse's strong hands felt so good that I did relax, which was the goal, but I relaxed so fully that—facedown with my head in the padded ring—I heard a small splat, and my eyes flew open to see that the sheet I was lying on was soaked with breast milk, now dripping to the floor. Good God. Of course while driving home I was stopped at a train crossing, a serious holdup in a town where trains took ten minutes to cross and came so frequently that I kept a paperback on the front seat. Anyway, when I got home and parked, before I even made my way up the walk, I could already hear that high-pitched, racheting, newborn squall. Tommy was holding her, pacing the porch, and when I climbed the steps he thrust the blanketed bundle at me and said, "Here, take it." Then he went inside to lie down because his stomach ached.

I haven't thought of this in a long time. Funny to think of it now that Claire's such a daddy's girl, as I wrote to you in my last letter.

We leave tomorrow for a last visit down to Tommy's folks in Mobile. School starts here shortly, dear K, and the students are arriving in town with their yellow U-Hauls. I've invited a few new M.F.A. students over tonight so they can meet each other. Sweet friend, I wish you could join us. I'm making mango margaritas, which I make once a year when mangoes go on sale three for a buck, which happened today, so the blender is on the counter beside a bowl of limes. If you could join us, I would fire you up a mean virgin margarita (well, maybe a small semivirginal one?), and we would be quite dangerous indeed. I think the smoking, overtaxed blender might never recover.

Love,
BA

August 2, 2004
Hi sweet Kathleen—

Sorry for writing this on the back of a House of Asia menu but we're on Highway I-49, headed for Mobile, and I've stupidly put my backpack in the trunk so I have no paper.

We just passed a curious billboard. It features a very tough, very broad-shouldered police officer, arms folded over his substantial chest, standing in front of his squad car on the side of the highway. The caption reads "I'm not your mama. Pick it up, Mississippi." An antilitter campaign, with this cop as poster child for the opposite of "your mama," who is a weak-willed, soft-brained doormat, the 3-D version of those garden stakes that show fat bottoms in bloomers.

Funny how a culture that claims to venerate mothers equates them so often with trash.

Kisses,
BA

August 4, 2004
Hi, Cutie—

We're in Mobile now, visiting Tommy's folks before we take Claire to New Orleans to see the aquarium. I understand they have a big tank of sea otters, one of my favorite animals. Sea otters have built-in pockets on their chubby thighs. If, say, they catch a fish, they can eat half of it now and save the other half for a snack later. No wonder they're so unquenchably happy.

I love getting Claire together with her grandparents. It's funny but there were times in high school and college when I wanted to live as far as possible from my mom—but now that Claire is here, I wish Mom lived in my backyard. We take Claire to Chicago a lot to see her, and when we do, my mom takes her to the Children's Museum or *The Nutcracker* or some form of big-city excitement. Tommy's folks in Alabama provide the perfect balance, country living where one can stroll to the backyard to pick satsumas and blackberries, and there are always a half dozen cousins, and animals, to play with.

This visit, Claire gets a special treat. An adopted stray cat gave birth to five kittens under the deck, and now they're two weeks old. It's so sweet to see them curled in my nephew's closet on a nest of towels, still so shaky they can walk only a few steps. I love to see the mama kitty roll over on her side and those kittens, eyes closed, nose their way to a teat, the same way that human babies do (I've read that babies as young as two weeks turn their head toward a lactating woman—so sensitive are they to the smell of milk). Anyway, one little kitty was blocked from its mama by its four brothers and sisters, who seemed to have everything all plugged up. It wriggled among the bodies of its siblings, squeaking. The mother lifted her head and mewed, but since the other four were already sucking she couldn't move much. So I lifted the body, as light as a dinner roll, and nudged it up against a free nipple, watched it knead the mother's tummy with its white forepaws and then suck furiously. Pretty soon they all were purring, the mother's contented purr at a lower register. I remembered how Claire would sometimes make "yummy" noises with my nipple in her mouth, and I ached a little.

Love,
Beth Ann

August 8, 2004
Dear One,

Just got your letter about the nightmares. When Claire was in
utero, I had every kind of nightmare possible, both sleeping and
waking. Mostly I'd dream about giving birth to a monstrous baby.
I'd look down to see my newborn daughter's face bulbous and
malformed, her eyes slid down her cheeks like melted candles,
her tongue poking through her cheek. Or I'd dream that her heart
was attached to the outside of her chest, pulsing translucently
like the throat of a frog. Only my monthly doctor's visits could
calm me, hearing the car-wash whoosh of her heart. For a few
days after, no nightmares. Then the old doubts would rouse
themselves, get a cup of coffee, circle my chair where I was reading. The next week, they'd be pulling my hair, kicking the chair
out from under me . . . finally it was all I could do not to call the
doctor and beg for an earlier appointment.

One time late in my pregnancy I watched a nature show about
baboons. It opened with the mother baboon stroking the wrinkled head of her newborn. Then the voice-over said that the
females help raise each other's young, but that baboons could be
jealous. New mothers had to be especially vigilant against
"maiden aunts." The camera focused on such an aunt, taking her
turn holding the infant. She ran her four long fingers down the
baby's hairless tummy while the mother began to forage a bit.
The mother looked over her shoulder, assessed the scene of famil-

ial contentment, and foraged a little farther away. The aunt kept stroking, stroking. Close up on her face: stealthily, cartoonishly, she looked both ways, tucked the baby under her arm like a football, and took off. The mother and the other baboons gave chase and cornered the aunt, who scampered up a tree. Shrieking and pounding the forest floor, they surrounded the tree. Finally the frustrated aunt slapped the baby upside the head and tossed it fifteen feet down into the outstretched hands of the mother. After watching that show, I dreamt all night that I gave birth to a healthy baby—which my sister stole.

You ended your letter with: "I can't wait until the baby's born and I can stop worrying so much, right?"

Well, buttercup—spoiler alert, as they say in entertainment magazines when they give away a movie's surprise—your fears grow right alongside the baby, ounce for ounce. They enter a new stage as she enters a new stage, they stretch as her body stretches, as your heart stretches. I worried about miscarriage until Claire was born, worried about SIDS when all she could do was lie in her bassinet. When she started crawling I stopped worrying about SIDS—but then I worried about her choking on something she picked off the floor. Then she learned to walk, and my delight in seeing her take those wobbly journeys was 90 percent joy, 10 percent: if she fell in this direction, she'd hit the coffee table, in that direction, the andirons. Now she walks steadily, and I can't be near a street—no matter how tightly I grasp her hand—without envisioning a car running a red light and hitting her. Wherever we go, we're tailed by her sister-specter, Death. Because we carry the sense of peril just as surely as we schlep that diaper bag.

Our vigilance can be taxing, but there is a happy side to this. Because we can't take our eyes off our babies, we don't miss the things we'd miss if we could look away. You'll see your baby change every day. Your impassioned observation is your homage.

Love,
Beth Ann

August 13, 2004
K,

Women who are very pregnant women have an underwater quality. I wish I could see you now in month seven, for I bet you have it, too. Oh the very pregnant underwater women, thick-lidded, woolly-brained, slow-limbed silent creatures spooling and unspooling, casting off the fitted clothes and the pointed shoes and the rings that cinch the swollen fingers until finally the women are all fluid finning and tentacles of silk scarves . . .

Such women remind us that humans, like mother earth, are

three-fourths water. And the ocean is made of the same elements as our blood—sodium, potassium, and calcium—and almost in the same ratio. The slooshy, leaky bodies of very pregnant women . . . where three or four are gathered, they should swim, for inside of them are tiny people, swimming, at five and six weeks these embryos even have tails, and inside of the girl babies already the eggs to create new babies slosh in their saltwater cellular pockets, the buoyant primordial soup of the living . . .

Love,
Beth Ann

August 16, 2004
Dear One,

The brassy sounds of summer's end trumpet at my window—here at my desk I can hear the high school marching band. The local schools convened this week, and Ole Miss starts on Monday. Oh, it's been a glorious, languorous summer, reading poems, trying perhaps to write one, scribbling you a letter, eating a big lunch, watering the flowers, going to the gym, picking up Claire, fixing her a snack, rolling with her on the floor, reading *Sing, Sophie, Sing!* or *Trout, Trout, Trout,* making a dinner with vegetables from the farmers' market, opening a bottle of wine that Tommy and I continue drinking as we take turns pushing Claire on the swing, or chasing lightning bugs with her, or cracking open a watermelon on the patio and eating the heart, the three of us bent over it with fingers and spoons, and when there's very little left, hosing the seeds and juice into the grass—then the long preparation for her sleeping, more books and songs, then lights-out as she squeezes Bunny while Tommy and I soft-foot down the hall to the couch where we finish the wine and talk about the day we had, the day to come.

Starting on Monday, you'll understand if my letters are briefer, no?

But while there's time, I want to answer that question you've asked twice now, why I delivered naturally. I've been putting off answering, partially to figure out what I need to say, partially because I know it will take me the better part of the day to write it down.

My daughter came into the world in Galesburg, Illinois, about a year after you left that prairie town. Because you lived in a dorm, and for less than a year, perhaps you didn't know many people in Galesburg, who are like the farms they live on—hardworking and practical. In the hospital, in the day or two after delivering, women walk the hallways leaning on the arms of sisters or mothers to get their systems running smoothly again. Pausing in front of the nursery glass, they trade birth stories. And when they heard mine, they eyed me. In the months before delivery, I had studied Lamaze, practiced breathing techniques and visualization in order to deliver my daughter without painkillers. And though the delivery turned out to be complicated, I managed. But I knew I looked pretty beat-up. Then one woman asked a question which, though simple, I still haven't answered to my satisfaction: "Why didn't you take the drugs?"

Why, indeed? The medical professionals kept offering them; "You don't have to feel a thing!" one nurse promised. The easy answer is that it's usually best for the fetus if the mother doesn't take drugs because they pass through her uterus. The baby may be born sluggish and unresponsive and could even have problems sucking, which impairs breast-feeding and bonding. But, to be practical, doctors can administer the drugs so late that only a very small amount passes to the baby. And even the drugs that do pass to the baby haven't been shown to have a lasting effect. So there's only a small risk to the baby from the drugs, but obvious benefits to the mother, which returns me to the question, why didn't I take them? An epidural would have made the birth easier on me—and certainly easier on poor Tommy, who came away from the three-hour pushing stage ready for an epidural himself. And after all, I'm no enemy of technology (aside from letters to you, I do most of my writing on a laptop) or of shortcuts (I eat salad from a bag; several boxes in my pantry proclaim "just add water").

So my decision to have a natural childbirth was only partly influenced by what would be best for Claire. I was also thinking about the birth experience I most desired: to be fully awake and alive to the experience I would undergo, even though it would involve tremendous pain. I didn't want to deaden the pain if it meant deadening the other emotions that would accompany the pain. I thought then, and still believe now, that being responsive and responsible to my experience would make it a better one.

Oh, it's a strange dilemma we modern women have, really. In previous generations, one didn't have the option of "choosing" how to deliver—all childbirth was "natural," and the numbing of labor pains, or any pains, simply wasn't possible. But in 1847 a doctor named James Young Simpson placed a handkerchief dabbed with chloroform over the nose of his laboring patient. The woman, whose previous delivery had involved three days of intense labor, delivered a healthy child in less than an hour. When she woke later, she had a hard time believing the doctor when he told her she'd already given birth.

Thus began the marriage of childbirth and medication, and for many it's been a happy marriage. By 1853, painkillers were being marketed widely for all sorts of medical procedures, and our relationship to pain changed. No longer did people have to suffer through their pain—but this also means that no longer could such suffering lead to enlightenment, or let the sufferer participate in the act of returning to health.

Don't get me wrong, there are times when anesthesia is not only helpful but a blessing. You witnessed your mother's last months, so you know this better than anyone. But it's also true that in many situations we can tolerate more pain than is commonly acknowledged, and there may be benefits in doing so.

The way the medical establishment treats pregnant women seems a metaphor for the way our industrialized, anesthetized culture treats all its citizens—we are offered drugs as the first solution. We become so used to the quick fix that any pain—sometimes even the pain of daily existence—needs to be numbed. Anesthetics, including the anesthetic of alcohol, are accepted as a sustained response to the waking world, a way of coping with daily life. However, "anesthetic" means "without aesthetic," that is, without the skills to create the sensory impressions that make daily life meaningful.

Continually "taking the edge off" interferes with the job of all humans, which is to engage in the world in all its complexity and find meaning there. And this job description expands when we enter motherhood, for we become responsible for more than our own events and emotions. Our children look to us to observe and interpret the world for them. "Tell me a story, tell me a story," Claire begs ten times a day. The stories we tell, and the stories our actions and relationships tell, combine to form *The Story of the World* that our children adopt as their own. As they grow, they can amend and revise this story, but never delete it. That is the power of the story, and its danger.

The interpreting role of the mother becomes particularly important when the child feels confused or fearful, such as when there's a sickness or death in the family. We have to come to terms with these painful events, for our children will ask us to. Claire's favorite word, like most three-year-olds, is "Why?" When I give an unexamined answer to my little thought-forming creature—their amazing brains learn ten words a day!—I hear it baldly. If my answer is glib or ironic or shallow, I hear it, and she must, too.

So I can only say, both as a sufferer undergoing a transformative experience and as a person interested in interpreting the events in the world, a natural childbirth was best for me. My decision reflects a larger philosophy, I suppose—that we are obligated to feel what we're feeling. I believe that understanding and articulating our suffering helps us understand and articulate our joy.

To return to the delivery room, studies have shown that there's a direct link between a mother's feeling of involvement with the birth and her level of satisfaction with that birth. And because a mother is less involved when she is *told* when to push, as opposed to feeling the urge to push, deciding against anesthetics can improve her happiness with the outcome. So I do think the brutal joy that cracked my heart open when the midwife laid my bloody daughter upon it was, in fact, connected to the pain I experienced during her delivery.

I hope all of this makes sense to you. It's been good for me to try to make sense of myself, to myself, as I've written you. But K, the most important thing for you to know is that it was *my* decision, and in a few months, you will make your own. Please don't feel pressure to do as I did. There are too many people out there who think their way is the right way, which it might be—and their way is the only way, which it is not. If there's one thing I can say for certain about motherhood, it's that it is a transformation which is deeply individual.

Love,
Beth Ann

August 20, 2004
Dear One,

Heard an alarming report on National Public Radio this morning about the high rate of postpartum depression in America—one of ten mothers experiences it. The rate is much lower in countries where a medical professional provides postnatal care at the new mother's home. A recent UK study followed two thousand new mothers over a series of weeks as they were visited multiple times by a midwife, and found they were 40 percent less likely to report depression than their American counterparts. But despite the correlation between lack of social support and depression, the U.S. health care system doesn't provide home visits, or much postnatal care at all, really—American mothers visit the doctor just once in the six weeks following delivery. The United States also falls at the bottom of the world rankings for maternity leave. American mothers are, by law, offered twelve weeks' unpaid leave; compare this with Sweden, which provides ninety-six weeks' maternity leave, the first year of which is at 80 percent of salary. Not surprisingly, Sweden has a very low rate of postpartum depression.

I would love to see some statistics about postpartum depression in America prior to 1900, when midwives were the norm, for I bet the syndrome was less common. The midwife knew the family, had often delivered the mother's previous babies and knew the workings of her body. In the days before delivery, the midwife moved into the household to observe and guide. Even after the delivery, she remained for a few days, restoring order in the house, helping the mother's milk to come in, administering poultices to the mother's healing body.

The prevalence of midwives decreased in the beginning of the twentieth century, when the scientific reform of medicine was called for. Medical schools sprang up to standardize education and laboratory training. Women of course couldn't attend these schools, so they couldn't earn the newly required license. Practicing medicine without a license could get a midwife jailed. And so men started taking over the field of obstetrics.

I don't mean to denigrate progress. Of course I'm glad for the advancements doctors gain through education; I'm glad there are licenses, boards, residencies, the whole shebang. But looked at through the lens of history, obstetrics is a rather new profession, and is perhaps due for a correction. I read in the paper a few weeks ago that the national average for caesarean sections has reached 27 percent. How can it be that over one-quarter of births require emergency intervention and major abdominal surgery?

The training that our medical students pay so dearly for doesn't encourage them to see birth as a natural process with its own timetable, but as a medical episode that should be concluded as quickly as possible. I know that had I delivered Claire with an obstetrician instead of a midwife, I would likely have been told I needed a C-section. Many doctors are obliged to follow charts indicating that a mother can be in the pushing stage no longer than two hours, and Claire took three hours.

If Tommy and I can get pregnant here in Mississippi (and why does it seem to be taking so long in this fertile, fecund state where everything seeds and grows and breeds? Last night I dreamt that a faraway voice called me "Mommy! Mommy," and though I ran for miles through kudzu-covered hills, I couldn't find it)—if Tommy and I can get pregnant here in Mississippi, I'd like to use a midwife again, and this time try a home birth. I know that makes me sound like some tie-dyed, hemp-wearing hippie (I shave my legs! I drink Diet Coke!), but I'm more and more convinced that standard hospital care doesn't encourage the natural, baby-centered birth I desire.

By the way, K, the midwife in a community, back when communities worked that way, was also the "layer out," the person who'd come to the house to prepare the dead body for its laying-out in the parlor and later burial. That's comforting to me, that birthing and dying could take place where the process of daily living is taking place, wound into the fabric of our days, remind-ing us of where we've come from, and where we're going, and soon.

Love,
Beth Ann

August 26, 2004
Dear One,

Woke this morning, the first day of school, thinking again about Michelangelo. Specifically, of his late great sculpture, *Moses*, which he completed in 1513, although he began it in 1505—he had been pulled reluctantly from the commission by the pope, who wanted the Sistine Chapel frescoed. When he was finally able to return to his sculpture, Michelangelo worked pas-sionately. Sometimes, chiseling the marble late into the night, he even dreamed that it might come to life. At its unveiling, upon seeing the lifeless form, Michelangelo attacked the sculpture. Evidence of the attack remains for the careful observer. There's a chip in Moses's knee where Michelangelo hurled his chisel, screaming *"Perché non parli?"*—"Why don't you speak?"

Michelangelo dreamed of creating a life, someone who could breathe and walk. Dr. Frankenstein dreamed of something similar. But only women can bring forth a living creature. We do this with our bodies. We do this with our hearts.

Funny, isn't it, that men don't more often express jealousy about the capacity to give birth? Do you think, Kathleen, that they simply aren't jealous? Somehow, I can't imagine that. Instead, I believe they express their insecurity less directly. I'm thinking, for example, how female creative power, and men's envy of it, might account for the misogyny sometimes directed at women who produce not only children but creative work as well. How I've struggled, dear K, with my nemesis and friend, old T. S. Eliot. Such poetry! Such pettiness! How destructive the perversion of that great mind.

In Eliot's *The Waste Land*, the intellectual characters are all male. They're accorded added dignity because they speak in iambic meter, and they often are connected to characters from history or myth, and are ennobled by these allusions. The female characters certainly aren't intellectuals—one crassly discusses abortion in a bar, another spends a vapid hour before the dressing mirror in her boudoir. With one exception, the females speak in free verse and aren't linked to mythical heroes. We do have Fresca, however, who was a reader and writer. Eliot punishes her for this gender transgression—he describes her literary output in terms of bodily excretions. The only throne Eliot allows Fresca is the one in the bathroom; while sitting there, Fresca reads *Clarissa* to ease "her labour" as she produces her "needful stool." This section was later excised from the poem by Ezra Pound, but Eliot's misogyny makes me think of Joyce's quip that "*The Waste Land* ended once and for all the idea of poetry for ladies."

Luckily for us, we have examples of creative women who are doing it all, and with style. After all, the first poet to publish a book in the American colonies was Anne Bradstreet, a mother of eight! For myself, I keep a mental list of sane poets who have children and have written great books. It's longer than you'd think. I encourage myself with poems like this one by Sharon Olds, "The Language of the Brag." She writes,

> *I have done what you wanted to do, Walt Whitman,*
> *Allen Ginsberg, I have done this thing,*
> *I and the other women this exceptional*
> *act with the exceptional heroic body,*
> *this giving birth, this glistening verb,*
> *and I am putting my proud American boast*
> *right here with the others.*

I've been thinking that I'd like to copy for you some of the poems I keep close because they make me feel strong. In the hospital, Robert might read them to you while you're in early labor. I'll also copy the mixed tapes of female rockers that I planned to listen to while in labor. I didn't end up wanting music, however— I felt I needed silence to concentrate—but I listen to them now when I go running and they make me feel kick-ass and strong. I'll send along your "birth goddess package" soon, so a part of me will be with you to cheer you on. That would sound a lot sillier to me if I didn't know that in many, many cultures, friends of a laboring woman make offerings and keep a vigil while she gives birth. Even elephants do this; wild elephant herds are made up of females, and when a member goes into labor, the others stop their foraging and gather round in support, sometimes trumpeting their encouragement. When the baby is born, they use their trunks to help nudge it to its feet, and for days afterward they treat the mother tenderly and take pains to avoid trampling the infant.

I can't be there in person while you do that "exceptional act with the exceptional heroic body," but I won't let you go into this feeling alone. There's a world of wise women and a surfeit of good birthing mojo—trust that some is being sent your way.

Love,
Beth Ann

September 1, 2004
Dear One,

What a relief to know that you've entered the phase in which the child is viable, a modest word that doesn't convey the succor it gives—knowing that if (God forbid) the baby came today, it would likely survive.

It's funny because a pregnant woman spends so much time anticipating the baby leaving the womb, longing for it, impatient for it, but the truth is when the baby is finally born, it's strange not to carry it inside anymore, however much she's longed for precisely that. After my own delivery, after the vomiting and shaking down the length of my body and the tears (I've read that even sea turtles cry while laying their eggs, but it's more likely just saltwater secretions), when the nurses had taken Claire for those first tests—the Apgar, the weighing, the blood work—I felt, somehow, lonely. Worse than lonely; bereft. Enjoying her perfect companionship was second nature. *She was* my second nature. I was plural, two heads, four arms, four legs, two hearts pumping blood through their eight chambers. Now she was outside of me and never would be inside of me again, would be spirited farther and farther away from my body, already she'd been wheeled out of sight by the nurses, and my double heart was cleaved, cleaved and inadequate. Julia Kristeva has written that one of the first functions of language is to help children create mental pictures of their absent mothers that the children can use to soothe themselves. But what soothes the mother who hears the child's cry echoing down the hallway?

Four days after Claire was born, there was that first visit to the pediatrician. Well, of course I was souped up with hormones—you probably know that the word "estrogen" comes from the Greek *oistros*, for "insane desire." But when jolly Delois stuck that Hep-B vaccination needle into Claire's thigh, that mottled thigh smaller than my wrist, Claire screamed, and I wanted to as well. I was holding her still and rubbing her arm to calm her, and when she looked at me I swear her eyes looked *betrayed*. I cried huge tears, tears huger than my eyes, then laughed at myself and thought of a line from Beth Henley's play *Crimes of the Heart:* "Laughter through tears is my favorite emotion." Carrying the whimpering bundle to the parking lot, I whispered apologies into her see-through ear and realized that the cotton sleeper my four-days-sprung daughter wore was damp with tears, matching mother-daughter tears. *You're in the world of people now; you're theirs as much as mine.*

Love,
Beth Ann

September 3, 2004

Dear One,

I'm glad to hear you'll be back in Georgia by December, sweet friend. I don't envy you moving with a month-old baby in an Alaskan winter, but selfishly I'm happy I can visit you when school's out, before Christmas. I'll be able to hold your baby before he or she is two months old. Oh, you'll love Christmas more than ever, as if it were your first Christmas too—that, and flying on an airplane, and seeing snow—all these things become imbued again with wonder.

Can you see the Milky Way from Anchorage? In this culture, where John Ashcroft spends eight thousand dollars on red drapes to cover the bare-chested statue of Justice in the State Department, we're not supposed to talk about breast milk, of course, but that's how the Via Lactia got its name. Zeus was the ruler of the Greek gods and lived on Mount Olympus with his wife, Hera, the queen of the pantheon. But Zeus was unfaithful to Hera and fathered a son with a human woman. He knew his son, Hercules, wouldn't be immortal, so Zeus brought him to Hera, hoping that she'd suckle him and the boy could gain some of her strength. Hera knew only that Hercules had been abandoned. Not guessing that his father was Zeus, she took pity and suckled the baby. Hercules, preternaturally strong, suckled so enthusiastically that Hera's pain was unbearable. She yanked her breast from his mouth, and as she did, an arc of milk sprayed across the night sky. The milky diamonds remain; they are our stars. Look up—there they are.

Love,
Beth Ann

September 6, 2004
Dear One—

It's Labor Day, so we drove into Memphis to "Libertyland" amusement park. Claire rode her first ride, the Pirate Ship, which rocked from end to end high in the air. We were watching her from behind the gate, taking the opportunity to sneak some of her Day-Glo blue cotton candy, when we saw a panicky look on her face. As the ship rocked up she was scanning for us, but although we were calling she couldn't find us, and her look changed to terror. "Stop," I told the ride attendant, "Please stop the ride, my daughter is scared," and blessedly he did. "Mommy got you down," Tommy told Claire. "Yes, Mommy always helps when I be scared," Claire replied. Oh, sweet day. I kissed and kissed her cotton-candied face.

Tommy wanted to take a turn on the big roller-coaster so Claire sat on my lap as we waited; she was sweet and a little clingy, which I confess I enjoyed. The "Zippin Pippin," the world's second oldest roller-coaster, a rickety wooden thing, is perhaps surpassed in daring by the new steel roller-coasters, but not surpassed in charm. I told Claire about Elvis (the G version) because the Zippin Pippin was the King's favorite ride. According to the placard, he rented out Libertyland on August 8, 1977, and took ten of his friends there. He rode the Zippin Pippin for two hours straight, wearing his black jumpsuit and turquoise-studded belt. This was Elvis's last public outing—he died August 16.

You ask about Robert reading my letters. It's fine, sweetheart—feel free to share them if he finds them interesting. You know, Kathleen, I've never been good at keeping a journal—oh I have my poetry notebook of course, but I've never kept track of the day's events without trying to give them shape, rhythm, frames. Of course, one can make a journal into art—I think of Virginia Woolf, of Annie Dillard, of May Sarton—but there's the question of audience that I find a bit dodgy—were those women really just writing for themselves? Hmm, I'm unconvinced. Writing you, I have the ritual of a diary, but there is most certainly a reader, or really two: you at the oak table drinking your hot milk with honey, and the baby who's grown so big that your belly brushes the table edge, keeping you from pulling your chair in, giving you a backache. The baby who kicks when you play the blues, so while that child will be born into a permafrost, he or she will have heard the songs of your South.

Days. Days are where we live, says Philip Larkin. There's

something about being pregnant that makes each day momentous. You're constantly measuring, checking the guidebooks' time frames, today the baby is as long as a comma, today it could fit in a walnut shell, today it is as big as a jumbo shrimp . . . all of these images attending you the way Io attends Jupiter. Oh I love science's instinct for metaphors, though they all fail, because what's your baby like? Your baby is like nothing that's ever been created.

When I was pregnant, I was an information junkie, reading as much as I could about developing fetuses. Sometimes I learned more than I wanted to. I don't think I ever told you about the infant CPR class I took mid-pregnancy, thinking I'd learn all sorts of foolproof tricks that would guarantee my baby's safety. What I found out is that in some emergencies, precious little can be done. The drill for a choking infant involved flipping the dummy, a tiny silver inflated torso, facedown across my forearm, then patting its back. That's it? I wanted to ask. The Heimlich maneuver might crack its ribs, puncture its lungs, apparently. I wanted my money back. And my belief that there were sure ways of keeping her safe.

Sorry to hear about how tired you are. Don't feel guilty about the naps, though! Why shouldn't you be tired? You're growing bones and teeth, you're forging a liver and appendix, you're molding the spongy Play-Doh chunnels of the brain! You are making unique fingerprints, pixie prints that no one else can make, no one else will have. And inside you now, your baby opens its eyelids. Of course you're tired, girl. Of course you're seeing double.

Oh—I'll mention this in case you don't come across it else-where—if you are engorged when you start breast-feeding (I felt like I was strapped into a harness of fire), you might try putting cabbage leaves around your breasts. Somehow, they douse the heat. It's a bit like being back in junior high, slathering on a Noxzema mask, a cool blue crystalline shell that tingles to tell you it's working.

Love,
Beth Ann

September 14, 2004
Oh yes, dear one—

I too remember that incredible impatience to see the baby, to hold it at last, to be assured that the baby is safe, the baby is healthy, even that the baby is (a shallow worry, but an honest one) cute.

We should be marsupials. Kangaroos give birth to very tiny young, which then wriggle from the birth canal and crawl up the mother's stomach purely by instinct to the mother's pouch, where they hole up and ripen to maturity. What lucky mamas we would be then, able to peek in on them occasionally, gingerly, the way you check a cake without causing it to fall.

Or we should have see-through belly buttons, a little lighted window into the warm oven where we bake that sweet roll so high and firm.

Kisses,
BA

Dear One—

Today, September 17, is the anniversary of the day my first child, had it lived, should have been born.

Again I think of my conversation with Ian at Sewanee. How I wish there were some ceremony, some ritual, to mark this occasion, to connect me to the others who have such an anniversary, so I could draw strength from them, give them strength. Twenty percent of pregnancies end in miscarriage, one out of five couples. My friend Jesse Lee said that knowing this makes you realize how many women are living in a world of silent sorrow. Sometimes when I am in a group of women and looking around, I realize that at least one member must have known this suffering, and it births in me a compassion I shouldn't have had otherwise.

Some animals, too, have a need to mourn and remember lost members of their tribe. (How arrogant we humans are—so convinced that we're the only species with deep feelings!) Joyce Poole, the scientific director of Kenya's Amboseli National Park, describes in *Coming of Age with Elephants* witnessing a mother elephant grieve her stillborn. First, the mother tried to nudge her dead baby to standing, tried to revive it—the mother was in denial, just as humans often are in the first stage of grief. Poole writes that the mother finally succumbed to mourning. She stood slumped beside the infant body, trunk lowered, and appeared to be crying. "I will never forget the expression on her face, her mouth, the way she carried her ears, her head, and her body," writes Poole. "Every part of her spelled grief."

When a member of an elephant herd dies, other elephants tear branches with their trunks from nearby trees and drop them on the dead body, also covering it with leaves and clumps of grasses. Then they stand by, rocking from side to side, in a manner that seems distinctly dignified and solemn. We say that "elephants never forget," and in matters of the heart, it seems they don't. Elephants remember, on their long treks through a forest, the spot where a member of their family died the previous year. In a nature program I once saw, a herd was on the move to newer territory when, mid-journey, one female stopped, head and ears drooping, trunk curled. She stood for a long time in this apparent attitude of mourning. The other elephants stood by until the female was ready to move again. Only when the naturalists tracking the elephants checked with the previous team of naturalists did they learn that this elephant had stopped precisely where she'd delivered a stillborn calf the previous spring. Human mothers come to know and love their infants in the ten months' gestation period. How devastating for the African elephant, whose calf gestates for over twenty-one months, to see that offspring dead.

September 17. If I were still at Notre Dame, I'd walk to the willow-shaded lake and soften my steps to approach the grotto with the statue of the Virgin Mary. No matter what time of the day or night I went there, I would find people kneeling in prayer. I'd fold my dollar bill and insert it in the vertical slot, then select a thick white candle, tipping the glass jar that protects it from the wind so I could angle the long wooden match inside. When it was lit, I'd set my burning candle among the long racks of burning candles. And with slow steps walk away, turning at the grotto's exit to see the lights, hundreds of lights, mine indistinguishable among them, trembling wetly in the cave of stones.

I found solace there. Even when my relationship to the church grew troubled, even when I could no longer pray, I found solace there.

Love,
Beth Ann

September 18, 2004
Dear One,

This morning, as if in response to the letter I wrote yesterday, I found in a book of ancient Greek poems this one by Bakchylides, written in the fifth century B.C., that is, twenty-five hundred years ago:

> Our sweet child, lifeless, woke
> in us that woe that none may speak.

How devastating is that first line break. And how all these labors connect the human race.

Love,
Beth Ann

September 22, 2004
Dear One,

I'm sorry it's taken me a bit to answer the question you asked in your letter of September 10. I do think you should tell your child that Robert's mother committed suicide. I know Robert's father would prefer if you didn't, but I've learned that family secrets, even those maintained to spare the feelings of children, have a way of festering. I'll explain a bit more what I mean.

I come from a family of small talkers. We could discuss the floral altar arrangements the whole fifteen-minute drive from church. The weather was fodder for a three-hour road trip. "Contributing to the dinner conversation" meant selecting from the cache of pleasant family anecdotes—my sister running from the school bus convinced that crows were trying to carry her away, me falling asleep in my plate of spaghetti. This is why I have never dreaded going to a gathering where I didn't know anyone. My whole childhood was a gathering where I didn't know anyone.

The closest I came to a sex talk, for instance, was in fifth grade when the moms came to school to watch their daughters watch a film on menstruation. Afterward, we were told, each mom would answer questions. So while the credits rolled, my mother and I found our assigned chairs. "Well," she asked after a few moments, "do you have any questions?"

"What's a virgin?" I asked.

"Why, did somebody call you that?"

"No, it's from a book."

I didn't say I'd been reading Judy Blume's forbidden *Deenie* in the bathtub. Later, my mother would walk in on me, and I would drown *Deenie* under the bubbles, then cough up thirty hard-earned babysitting dollars to the Lake Forest Library for a new one.

Now my mother paused, considering. "I don't know," she finally offered. We spent the rest of our time chatting about my math teacher's new haircut.

My ignorance about sex didn't cause me harm, but my ignorance about other matters did. I never heard my father talk about his brother, or mention how he died. My cousin revealed that this uncle had been an alcoholic who, after leaving his wife, drank himself to death. The occasion for this revelation was the funeral of my father, who had also left his wife and drunk himself to death. Knowing my uncle's fate might have helped me discern a pattern, but unpleasant things simply weren't discussed. Meanwhile, the TV showed drunks as homeless men drinking Colt 45s from brown bags. So when my handsome, hardworking father came home and drank a six-pack or two, when his words grew woolly and someone flicked the dimmer on his eyes, he was, as my mother said, tired.

Out of frustration with pleasant trivialities, I turned to reading. The big brick house where I grew up was a hundred years old and had no air-conditioning, but it was just down the street from the library. Oh, the summer of the heat wave—the summer my father finally got central air installed—when I would walk to the beautiful domed building and push open the massive doors into the cool, cool air and descend the marble steps—steps so old they were bowed in the middle—to the children's library with its posters urging us on to the classics, with its kid-sized chairs and kid-height water fountains, with Mrs. Krakora's desk where you'd sign out the giant bathroom key to use the tiny potty.

I fell in love with reading because in books things happen for a reason. I bet you can recall me saying in class that good endings are "surprising yet inevitable"; even the plot twists and reversals are prepared for. Not so with life. My sister and I were teenagers when my father's pharmaceutical company downsized and he lost his high-paying job, but we weren't warned that this might happen, and weren't told when it did. We'd never discussed money in my house and didn't do it then, but I realized something was wrong when my clothing allowance (yes, we were that spoiled) didn't appear on my desk. I found out what was wrong by reading the paper. Years later, when my parents got divorced, we were again completely unprepared, having seen none of the wrenching and elaborate rituals my friends' parents underwent prior to divorcing, like marital counseling and trial separations. I thought my parents would be married forever: I had never seen them argue. Then, one strangely silent morning, I carried the folded laundry upstairs. With a stack of my father's undershirts in my arms, I toed open the cedar door of his armoire. And found it empty.

In *The Glass Anvil*, Andrew Hudgins confesses "The Lies of the

Autobiographer," and one of them is "narrative cogency." This occurs when the author excises extraneous details and characters, "the narrative underbrush," so that the story, "like a flowering crab apple in a lot overgrown with sumac, can be more easily seen and appreciated." Because my family life was all chatter about the underbrush, I became addicted to the intensification and clarity that books provide. Many of my early memories concern books—the Multiple Sclerosis Read-a-thon, for instance, when I went door-to-door asking neighbors to pledge money for each book I'd read the next month. I don't know how many they thought I might finish—half a dozen?—when they pledged a dollar per book. Some of them weren't so glad to see me when I returned having read forty-seven. One cheapskate even quizzed me on plots, one after another, while I stood on his front step banging my clipboard against my knees.

Another early memory, one of my first, was waking from a nightmare and running, crying, into my parents' bedroom. "What will I do," I asked my mom, "when I'm done?"

"Honey, slow down, what do you mean? Done with what?"

Crying harder now. "When I'm done, what will I do? What will I do?"

She finally got it out of me, and my answer became the punch line of another recycled family anecdote: "When I'm done reading all the books in the world."

If I recall a childhood memory that doesn't involve a book, it was probably stolen from one. Sometimes I remember losing a baseball game or winning a spelling bee or getting a bad haircut from a beauty school trainee or waiting for my period to start—and I realize it never happened. I imagined it so convincingly I "painted" myself into it, the way Renaissance patrons would have their faces added to the background of Resurrection paintings.

I spent one preteen summer reading pick-your-own-ending books: *If you want Mindy to sneak into Amber's cabin and look for the trophy, turn to page 37; if you want Mindy to report the missing trophy to Counselor Jennings, turn to page 42.* And when I turned to page 37 or 42, I'd read until I could choose between two more options. I could even start the book over and make different choices, all logical. What a disappointment to be called to dinner where we could discuss the London broil for ten minutes but never once mention that my mother had switched wineglasses to trick my father into drinking less, shallow six-ouncers replacing the sixteen-ounce fishbowls designed for swirling cabernet. What I lacked was the clarity, the taut morality, of a pick-your-own-ending story: *Beth Ann's father is an alcoholic. If you want her to confront him, turn to page 37. If you want her to ignore it and run away to Eastern Europe, turn to page 42.* I couldn't see the plot of life—because of A, B happens to C—because I'd never heard of C and only knew half of A and it's best, dear, not to mention B. Without plot, events are ahistorical, there's no cause and effect, no climax or resolution. Without plot, shit happens.

After the long, long family dinners, I yearned to return to my book, while my mom stalled me by asking questions. I didn't understand, or didn't want to, that what she needed was company, not help with the dishes, before my sister and I went to bed and she was by herself, my father having passed out in his Holy Cross chair. Those times when she'd bend over my reading chair and smooth my forehead with the pad of her thumb, saying, "Don't concentrate so hard. You'll get wrinkles," she was wading out to where I was, pulling me back to the land of the living with her own warm flesh, since that's what it took. The deeper I was in—especially if I was lost enough to smile, or laugh, or cry—the more she couldn't help herself: "Hop up and fetch me my slippers, Beth Ann." I would be wrenched out, stunned and stupid, blinking, then dog-ear a corner of my paperback and put it down. Finally, my bedtime would arrive, and I'd be reading under the covers with a flashlight when I'd hear her try to rouse my father, then give up and trudge up the stairs. If the book I was reading was a very good book, I wouldn't even hear that.

With books I practiced escapism, and eventually I did escape. I ran away to Eastern Europe, and I stayed away for a good long time, and when I came back everything that was going to happen had happened. We were told an alcoholic needs to hit "rock bottom," but my father, overachiever to the end, drank himself to death before ever hitting any bottom rocky enough. His deterioration was very ugly, and very quick, though not so quick that he didn't squander all the family money first (an end to clothing allowances for all of us, forever). My mother, an Irish-complexioned beauty, grieved until her black hair fell out. My sister wore a mouth guard to bed because nightmares made her grind her teeth. And me? I turned to reading. But somehow, it went bad. The wheels fell off. I was desperate to lose myself, but I kept dragging my miserable self everywhere. The magical kingdom was closed.

The AA literature says that for alcoholics, drinking is a disease. They aren't to blame. It's been ten years, Kathleen, since my father ran away from home to drink himself to death. But I still haven't reconciled myself to his blamelessness. It's hard not to feel that he chose drinking over being my father. Hard not to feel that drinking was his greatest love, for which he made the ultimate sacrifice: dying. I struggle to stop blaming him, and I also struggle to acknowledge that I must bear some blame. For I grew too comfortable in that legacy of silence and detachment from the suffering of those closest to me. If I had risked more, if I had locked us all in a room and forced us to talk about our secrets and our fears, if I had been—I guess there's really no other way to say this—*a better person*, could I have saved us? I'll never know. My reading was complicit, and cowardly.

With books I practiced escapism, but it is also books that, in the end, led me back to my life. While reading can be deeply narcotic, it is also a drug that heals. For reading lifts us out of ourselves, and when we're returned, we're more empathetic, more capacious, wiser. I think reading can be a moral act.

Gradually, my reading took on a different quality, as I read not to drown my emotions but to towel them dry. For while we think our emotions are pure, fully formed, and logical, this is rarely the case. We must pay attention to them if we are to do justice to them and educate ourselves. I educated my soul through reading. I played with point-of-view, imagining other characters in the story, like my parents. Through this, I began to understand them, which softened me a little. As time went on I learned how events create plot, so when I felt that because my father made a mess of his life I was bound to make a mess of mine or marry someone who'd mess it up for me—well, eventually I had to admit this plot lacked the "inevitability" of a thoughtfully designed story. I understood at last that I really could choose my own ending.

I had one rule for dating men: they had to be more interesting than the book back on my night table. One such man came to dinner at my house, and brought me a book of Raymond Carver's poems, and read me "Hummingbird," which Ray wrote for his wife, Tess, before he died, and all the tenderness that was in that poem was in the giver of that book of poems, and now "Hummingbird" is engraved in our wedding bands. Yes, that book-bearer was Tommy, and we had ourselves a child, and, Lord, we do love her. Her first word (it sounds like a "lie of the autobiographer," but isn't) was "book." Not Mama, not Dada, but *book*. *Booook*, she said, not only when turning the chunky cardboard pages of *Guess How Much I Love You* but when finding anything made of paper; *Booook*, she said, ripping the TV guide, *Booook*, flinging the mail off the table, *Booook*, stuffing my grocery receipt in her mouth.

She is wading deeper into the world of language, which is both thrilling and terrifying. For sometimes books will confuse her, and she'll have questions. And she'll want to know what a virgin is, and maybe I can handle that, but she'll also want to know why I have no photos of her grandfather around. Truth is, it still isn't easy for me to discuss difficult subjects, though I think writing to you is helping. My background as a small talker and a slipper-fetcher and a nearly-entering-a-coma-reader makes me want to chat, dance, read until the "unpleasantness" goes away. But I need to answer her questions so that she knows it's okay to ask them, and so my father doesn't become to Claire what my uncle was to me, or what Robert's mother could become to your child—a treacherous absence. I need to answer her questions so that she doesn't come to think of silence as a minefield, or pleasantries as Band-Aids on a broken leg. I need to answer her questions so that afterward, if she opens a book, it's out of a desire to enrich her life, not obliterate it. Here on paper (*Booook*), for you, Claire Elizabeth Franklin, I pledge that I'll try.

Love,
Beth Ann

September 25, 2004

Again, dear one, I'm thinking how poetry and motherhood are similar. Because both take you out of your self, blur your boundaries. Here's Czeslaw Milosz, who died this month, in "Ars Poetica?": "The purpose of poetry is to remind us/how difficult it is to remain just one person." Become a mother and you are never just one person again.

Another similarity: both a baby and a poem masquerade as something we've created, when we know that they arrive from somewhere beyond us, that they are gifts. When the poetry is working, it doesn't feel so much that I'm crafting it as that it's presenting itself. Of course it's not often like this, but it has been— the bright ribbon of the poem unspooling in my mind and waiting while my fingers fasten it to the paper. I've had that. God, I've had that.

And it's the same with Claire, but more so. People look at her and they say, "Oh, she's so smart, so verbal!" They say, "What a delightful child." What do I say? I say, "Thank you." As if it were my doing. But really I want to say, I know! I can't understand it! From where did this creature arrive?

There's so much in her I can't take credit for. The past few days she's been calling me "Missy Gorio." I haven't understood what this meant, which has frustrated her. Last night, I was fastening the cape onto the Velcro tabs at the shoulders of her Batman pajamas—got them in the boys' section and we both adore them—and she again called me "Missy Gorio." For the first time I realized she meant "Commissioner Gordon." "Yes, Batman?" I asked her. And she threw her chubby arms around the neck of Commissioner Gordon, who kissed her happily before tucking her snugly into the Bat Cave.

Love,
Beth Ann

September 26, 2004
Dear One—

Oh, but they are beautiful: if our hair is blondish, their hair is golden. If our hair is wavy, theirs curls in perfect wood-shaving spirals. If we practice faith in alchemy, smoothing elaborate botanical extracts onto our skin, their bodies are the blooms and berries, their elbows and knees smoother than our expensive cheeks. Oh, but they are beautiful, their eyelashes long as giraffes', their enormous eyes transparent of guile, or, later, full of guile but unable to hide it and therefore charming—beautiful, beautiful creatures—

And *why* are they beautiful, Kathleen? They are beautiful so we don't kill them.

Love,
Beth Ann

September 30,
Dear One,

Just got your letter in which you say you're scared of the pain of childbirth. Well, that's just good sense. In regard to your questions, I hesitate to answer. On one hand, I don't want to scare you. But I think we do mothers great harm when we downplay the gravity and difficulty of giving birth. Here I'm thinking about a book I read during pregnancy in which the doctor spoke not of labor pain but of "discomfort." Later I recalled that bitterly, wished I could subject that doctor to a little discomfort of his own. This was the same book, I think, that included a diagram of the baby descending the birth canal, smiling.

Another book listed in a closing chapter the things a mother might consider packing in her bag for the hospital: "lip gloss, a tennis ball for back massage, and socks (dark in color)." Why "dark in color"? I wondered. It seemed a curious fashion tip. Later I realized it was because your feet in the stirrups get splattered with blood. But why not say that? Why not mention the blood? My God, there's so much blood, even the day after birth it is still leaking out. I understand that if you have an epidural they put a blood-clotting agent in your IV which helps slow down the flow. For me, the day after birth a nurse rubbed deeply, painfully on the deflated stretched sack of my belly to press out the jellied black blood clots. Later, the same kind nurse steadied me as I hobbled to the toilet; before the mother is released, the hospital wants her to have a bowel movement to make sure her system is running again. She lowered me gently while I grasped the handrails, and kept up a stream of chatter while I filled the toilet bowl with yet more blood and hoped my stitches would hold against the terrible pressure. All that she did for me, and I don't even know her name.

I am not going to call labor pains "discomfort," and if I tell you to pack dark socks, I'll tell you why. But I'll also tell you the other half of the story, the part that our soon-to-be-mothers need to know most:

You are a warrior. You are a warrior, and for your whole life your body has been warming up for this great fight. These last months have been consumed with training everything inside you, all of the hormones and the loosening of the joints have been in preparation for this, and you are ready. You know, more or less, the day, the place, of your battle, and you will meet it because you are destined for it, it is the greatest challenge your body will ever know. Oh we women needn't play at war and its games like men I've known who can't disguise their aggression and excitement when the bombs begin falling on some country or other. We needn't play at war because if we give birth, we go to war, and at the deepest level, deeper than bone-deep, our evolutionary history tells us that it's a matter of life or death.

We women are hard, hard on our bodies. We've been taught to look at them as an assemblage of trouble spots, a miasma of flaws. But we've been all wrong! Think of the ordinary, remarkable things your body has done. Your hands? You have pressed them deep into the yeast-warm dough and punched it down, let it rise until doubled in size and punched it down again. Your hands have, hundreds of times, fit themselves into Robert's, your fingers meshing like the teeth of a zipper. Your legs? They have walked you through the peach orchards of In Between, Georgia, and between the row houses of Atlanta's Cabbage Town. They have run you into the salty buoyant waves of the Gulf which have struck your sternum until you dove through one and let your body be carried. You have run and you have jumped and you have fallen and bled and seen your body heal itself. You have dug six-inch-deep holes in the autumn loam to plant the bulbs of bearded iris and you have cooked feasts and filled your belly with them and you have taken the loved part of your loved man deep inside and you have forged this creature from star-stuff and now you will battle to set it free. You are stronger than you know. You will split open your body to free the tiny god who will be caught and held up like a hero. You are the hero. No one but you can do it. Rich women or poor women—in labor, they are equally unencumbered. Women alone or women surrounded by loved ones—in labor, at the end, they are equally alone. No doctor will deliver your child. You will deliver your child, and you will be delivered.

Remember this when the contraction comes and your whole belly tightens like a shell about to be cracked. All the muscles in your belly, muscles you don't remember having, will grow rigid and fused like the carapace of the ornate box turtle. After some moments, it will pass, your muscles unclench, and again your flesh will feel like a taut sail propelled by more wind than it can take without tearing, but still your flesh. Then you know it won't be long until your ordinary, miraculous flesh, your warrior body, will be victorious.

Love,
Beth Ann

October 1, 2004
Dear One,

Funny to get your letter about craving collard greens in today's
mail because I've been struggling all morning with an assignment
for the Southern Foodways Symposium. The Foodways folk are a
group of Southern restaurateurs, food enthusiasts, food writers,
and lovers of Southern culture who seek to preserve Southern
foods, methods of cooking, and stories about food. I guess, to
put it simply, they use food as a lens to examine Southern culture. My pal John T. Edge directs the conference they have here
in Oxford every fall, and he asked me to come up with "a feast of
words" about Southern cuisine to open the Saturday morning
conference session.

I said yes months ago in the swelter of summer when October
was a mirage. Now the conference is a week away and I haven't
come up with anything—maybe because I'm still trying to work
out exactly how I fit in the South. I'm shy to write about Southern
foodways when some audience member might bust me as a
Yankee interloper.

And *am* I a Yankee interloper? When I first came to the South,
I was twenty-four and heading to the University of Arkansas to
get my M.F.A. in poetry writing. My family in Chicago kept talking about my move to the "Deep South" with wonder and trepidation—to them, yuppified Fayetteville in northwest Arkansas
was just down the river from *Deliverance* country.

While I was making my trip South, Tommy was leaving his home in Alabama to head to the same university on his first trip "way up North," as his family called it, also with wonder and trepidation—for them, Fayetteville was just down the road from the gang warfare of St. Louis.

Here's the short version of what happened next: we met and we fell in love, and I never really went back North again.

Understanding my new home in the South meant, of course, coming to understand its foods. I easily adopted grits, fried okra, and sweet potatoes. But these were rather superficial adoptions; mostly I ate and cooked what I have always eaten and cooked. That's not acculturation. Acculturation, as acculturated folks know, involves pain. My story of acculturation begins with an innocent offer: what type of cake would Tommy like for his birthday? I think you'll remember that I make wonderful cakes, probably because I have a determined sweet tooth so I've grown cagey about gratifying it. Invite me to a dinner party, for example, and I'll not ask, "Can I bring something?" but "Can I bring dessert?" which prevents the postprandial surprise of the host passing sliced strawberries. Strawberries, Kathleen, unless dipped in white chocolate, are not a dessert, they're a *garnish*. Dessert means chocolate, preferably dark, what someone with a less distinguished palate might call "too rich." So would Tommy perhaps enjoy my chocolate almond ganache with crème anglaise? My bitter chocolate hazelnut torte? Dacquoise? Génoise? Anything that rhymes with "awes"?

"Um, how about red velvet?" he asked.

"Um, sure," I replied. But not only had I never heard of this concoction, I couldn't find it in either my batter-splatted *Elegant Desserts* or *The Cake Bible*. Finally I went to the Source: my future mother-in-law, who was glad to share the recipe. Now that I think of it, perhaps it was that phone call that began our deep friendship, because Betty saw that her son's Yankee girlfriend wanted to make him happy.

But there was a *problem* with the recipe. More than one, in fact. First, when I sprinkled the vinegar on top of the baking soda, it hissed at me. The cakes I baked did not require safety goggles. The cakes I baked did not talk back. I discovered the second, bigger problem when the batter was almost finished and I realized just how much red food coloring was in the four-ounce bottle the recipe called for. Should I phone again and ask my potential mother-in-law to recheck her recipe? "The cake's supposed to be dark red," Tommy said.

"How red?" I asked.

"You know, like a dead armadillo on the roadside." And I'd been in the South *exactly* long enough to know how red that was.

All my sweet husband-to-be wanted for his birthday was a red velvet cake, but, I confess, he didn't get one. I tried—Lord knows I tried. But as the bottle of food coloring hovered over the batter, my hand just couldn't commit to tilting. What was in this stuff anyway? I brought the bottle close: propylene glycol, propylparaben, and FD&C Red #40. I let three fat drops fall into the batter, stirred it to a lovely cherry-blossom pink, then shoved the pans in the oven.

And so July 7, 1995, the pink velvet cake was born. I have made it each July 7 since for Tommy's birthday. The last three years, I've also made it May 19, our daughter's birthday. Claire, unlike her mama, has never known anything but Southern cuisine. Her first solid food was sweet potatoes, and her favorite vegetable is "fried Oprah." Claire enjoyed her first dessert, like most babies, at her one-year birthday party. At that point, Claire's little rosebud palate was pure of processed sugars, not to mention FD&C Red #40. When the moment for her debauchery arrived, I held up the baby fork with a crumb of the cake on it. She stuck out a tentative tongue, touched the icing, then slipped her tongue back in her mouth. An expectant hush overtook the solemn party guests wearing conical hats. Then, as if the glorious gates of sugar-rush paradise trumpeted open before her, Claire leaned forward in her high chair and, with both hands, yanked the fork into her mouth. Next she was tearing into the cake with both fists, smearing cake up her nostrils and into her eyelashes. The following morning, as I got Claire ready for the day, I was reliving the memory of a party so successful that its cleanup involved swabbing Q-tips in my daughter's ears. But as I began to change her diaper, I felt a panicked sickness at finding a bloody mess inside of it. I was heading for the car to take Claire to the doctor before I realized it was just the red food coloring.

Of course, all of this brings up a thorny question—by adapting Southern food and foodways for my New South family, am I merely diluting them, bleaching them, producing pale pink when crimson is called for? Perhaps. But I also know that healthy traditions can accept adaptations, in the same way that healthy animals and plants systems do, and in the same way language does, for we think of language as a closed system, but it is no fossil, it is an organic, seething marvel, continuously created and re-created, tumbling into the future with its bundle of blanks and redundancies. The only languages that are perfected are those that are dead. And if I've learned one thing living in the South, Kathleen, it's that Southern cuisine is anything but dead.

Back to my story now: Girl meets boy. Girl meets delicious Southern Boy, and they have themselves a delicious Southern Child. Well, where does that leave the Girl? I know, as much as I'd like to call myself one, I'm not a Southerner. But I'm also no longer a Yankee, at least not the kind my husband was warned against. Oh, I don't claim to admire everything about the South, or understand it—I still think the term "Fry Daddy" sounds more like a rapper's handle than a kitchen appliance. And my thighs hope it stays that way. But I'm learning where I fit in the South, and where the South fits in me. Learning what to adopt, and what to adapt. And learning that, sometimes, one moves through the pain of acculturation to come out on the other side in a rainbow of pleasure.

And if those Southern Foodways folks don't believe me, they should stop by my house May 19 or July 7 for what I guarantee is the best pink velvet cake they've ever had.

Look, darling—in writing to you about why my place in the

South is hard for me to write about, I think I've come up with something I can use in my talk. How sneaky is the subconscious.

Meanwhile, hang in there—a few more months and you'll be back in the land of collards and butter beans and black-eyed peas, where even the local Piggly Wiggly has a bin of boiled peanuts. In the meantime, I'm including in this package a bag of stone-ground grits for you three to enjoy some Alaskan morning when you need a little Southern sunshine in your bellies.

Love,
Beth Ann

October 5, 2004
Dear One,

Had a terrible time getting Claire to sleep last night, because I'd forgotten her blanket in Arkansas, where we spent the last few days giving readings. Somehow, in the rush of packing and unpacking at different houses, we left it behind. Tonight we didn't get home until past her bedtime, and Claire was so tired that not having the blanket really pushed her over the edge. My attempts at a substitute only made her more angry. She was crying, "I want my blankieee . . . I want my blankieee . . ." long after I went to bed myself. I felt like a rotten mom.

I know in many ways Tommy and I are lucky that our jobs are so flexible, that we can often keep Claire home from preschool, or take her on trips that, while interesting and fun, are also trips we get paid for (modestly). And I know part of the reason Claire is so verbal is because she meets so many different kinds of people, spends a lot of time with adults.

Yet sometimes I worry that the life we're providing doesn't have enough structure. How many dozens of guest rooms has she bedded down in at the age of three. How often her schedule gets switched around, with her meals and naps early or late or cut entirely. We're raising her in a house where every weekend brings a new houseguest that she gets attached to and receives a present from, but might not see again before she forgets she ever knew that "aunt" or "uncle." At dinner, when other children ask to say the blessing, Claire asks to make a toast. Recently, I was trying to teach her when to use the singular "child" or the plural.

"Claire," I asked, "when one friend comes over, what do you have?"

"A child," she said.

"Good. And when two friends come over, what do you have?"

"A party!" she replied.

Even when we're home and it's just us, our schedule changes day to day, week to week. Even our finances change—either it's summer and we're hardly getting paid and we're eating ramen noodles and drinking Busch, or the mail brings an unexpected royalty check for Tommy and then it's Lobster Gram and the King of Beers.

Once again, I want to do right by my child—if only I could feel 100 percent certain what the right thing is. During the long drive home from Arkansas I thought about this, knowing there would be two or three days before her blanket could arrive. I watched her in the rearview as she rocked out in her car seat to our crazy music—she'd asked for the Ramones' "Blitzkrieg Bop" by name, sang along to the Clash's "Should I Stay or Should I Go," head nodding like a bobble toy. When she looks back on her childhood, will she wish for stability, routine? Will she wish for Raffi?

One thing that comforts me—remembering how last fall Tommy and I drove to Little Rock to see Lucinda Williams in concert. God, she is amazing, her voice like silk tearing on a rusty nail. That night, in front of her hometown crowd, she rocked especially hard; she was raised not too far away in Fayetteville by Miller and Jordan Williams, who were in the audience. Miller, a great poet, had been one of my professors at the University of Arkansas, and has been a big support to me. Anyway, between two songs, Lucinda paused and started talking about what a wonderful upbringing she had, although it was nontraditional. In front of that big crowd, she thanked her parents for the job they did, and thanked them for playing good music when she was growing up, and recalled as a very young girl listening to the Fugs. So maybe there's hope for Claire yet.

Love,
Beth Ann

October 8, 2004
Dear One,

Got Claire out of bed a while ago and found a cigar, still in its plastic sleeve, in her crib—a strange souvenir from when Tommy checked on her last night. In the striped light of the moon filtering through her blinds, I imagine, he leaned over the crib and the cigar slid from his breast pocket.

Now the two of them are outside on the swing set—sweater weather is here at last, and the high school marching band practicing down the street comes more clearly since the first leaves have fallen from the tops of the trees—and I've stolen time to answer your letter which arrived yesterday. I'm sorry to hear about the new doctor. Something similar happened to me with a doctor in Galesburg, before I found Cindy, our midwife. Just a few minutes into this doctor's examination, he seemed impatient with my questions. He scolded me for not volunteering information about a vitamin I was taking, but interrupted me when I did try to speak. I don't recall him looking me in the eye—he scribbled notes in my folder when I was talking, then stood up to scrub his hands in the metal basin, and he concluded the examination with "Be good" tossed over his shoulder like a bone. I felt like a child, not like someone who planned on birthing one.

I think a lot of women feel frustrated with the doctor-patient relationship because it's so hard to enter it on equal footing, especially with the more traditional doctors. The mother-to-be sits in her rustling paper gown, addressed by her first name by the fully clothed doctor, usually male, who is addressed with his professional title, backed by a wall of diplomas. So if she hears some advice she doesn't understand, or something he suggests goes against her instincts—well, it's hard to find the courage to question. Some of my friends have brought a doula into the labor room to advocate for the mother's wishes. A good idea, but doesn't this presume that the doctor might be unaware of—or acting against—the mother-to-be's wishes?

It's hard to know how to address the communication gap and the asymmetry in many of these relationships between older male obstetricians and their patients, who are necessarily female and usually younger. A book by Alexandra Dundas Todd called *Intimate Adversaries* helped me to see that a good deal of the frustration on both sides arises from different methods of communication.

Sociologists report that in the weeks after a mother gives birth, she feels almost a "physical compulsion" to tell her story. A quick glance at any of the parenting chat rooms bears out this study anecdotally—there's even a Web site, BirthStories.com, dedicated to this endeavor. Obstetricians, however (especially male ones), prefer to ask questions and receive answers, a leading reason why obstetric visits can be difficult for both doctor and patient. The satisfaction of the new mothers, according to Todd, is "dependent on their being able to tell doctors stories in their own words—their understanding of what is going on in their own or their children's lives." I think it makes sense that the mothers feel the "facts" belong in a larger setting, a more holistic, integrated context, because stories are how we shape our lives, and stories make pain tolerable by acknowledging it as part of a meaningful journey.

Well, sweet friend, I join you in hoping that your regular doctor is available when your big day arrives. Just a few weeks now. Go on and get that pedicure you've been talking about. And send a photo of your glorious belly for my bulletin board.

Love,
Beth Ann

October 11, 2004
Dear One,

Tunafish on Doritos? When I was pregnant, I wanted butter-
scotch malted milks. There was a roadside stand a few miles away
that made them thick and sweet. "Tommy," I'd call, too pregnant
to get off the couch without a reason and a boost, "the baby
wants a milkshake." And we'd both smile—how could he deny
this request? Then he'd be in the hallway screwing on his too-
tight Braves hat and fishing the keys from the fruit bowl.

I haven't had a malted milkshake since. I know it couldn't pos-
sibly taste as goldenly good as it did in those first hot days of
summer, the salad days in the old brick house in Galesburg where
I lay on the couch beneath the fan, one hand cupping the globe
of my belly with its map of veins, the other drifting through the
pages of a baby magazine, listening for the Nissan turning into
the gravel drive, home from Big Bob's Dairy Stand.

Have you ever read or seen the play *The Duchess of Malfi*, written by John Webster in the 1620s? It maintains that denying a
pregnant woman's cravings could be disastrous—her baby could
come out looking like the food that she'd craved. The baby of
one unsated woman came out looking like a cauliflower. I think
some very clever women came up with this superstition to ensure
that their cravings were indulged, don't you?

Meanwhile, here in MS, I'm thinking about pancakes. My
mom is visiting this week and Claire and I are the first ones up—

we'll start the batter soon. My mom would have gotten up with Claire if she'd heard her first, so this would have been a good morning to sleep in, but I couldn't help waking at six-thirty, like I always do. My sleep habits are just another way I've changed irrevocably since becoming a mommy.

I used to be a famously deep sleeper. When I first woke in the morning, I'd go for ten, twenty minutes without moving. Tommy compared me to a newborn puppy that doesn't open its eyes for several days. At night, if he came to bed after I was already asleep, he found me pliable, could arrange me for perfect snuggling or spooning and I'd never wake, never sigh or groan. Being a deep sleeper was a luxury, and a talent. Once a houseguest said of my morning slowness to converse: "She's got a long runway."

But all of this changed with Claire. Changed overnight, as they say. Suddenly I roused at her least whimper, out of bed and in her room before Tommy even stirred. Each night's dreams read less like a novel, more like a series of short shorts. I became another mother in her nightgown rocking her baby, staring out the window cornered with frost into the black night growing gradually bluer. No longer the sleepy puppy, I took my place at the end of a line, headed by foremothers who slept in caves with their little ones wrapped in furs, mothers who sprang awake to make sure the child wasn't being sniffed by some hungry beastie. And I can't return to my old ways—even nights when I'm away from Claire, my ear still listens, my body still wakes when she would be waking.

I miss sleeping in, miss waking slowly, dream swollen. Miss the way Tommy could arrange my limbs for his perfect comfort and snuggle with me all night, how we'd turn together like pages in a neverending book. Now I wake when he shifts in bed, wake when he coughs. But I understand too that I can't return to the old me because I've been awakened permanently, baptized into a new life, this good life, motherhood.

Go on now, eat your tuna on Doritos, before your baby comes out looking like a fish, or an ear of corn. And bon appétit.

Love,
Beth Ann

October 16, 2004
Dear K,

Has your belly button popped out? Ah, the pregnant belly button: the knot of an overblown balloon, its puckered mouth holding back too much air, the cheeks stretched thin with the effort. Or is it someone plugging a desperate finger into a chink in the Hoover Dam—watch out, it's gonna blow. Or the turkey tester which shows everyone just how done you are. My "outie" was so pronounced it looked like a toadstool, impossible to disguise beneath my maternity tents. But I enjoyed the comic-book silliness of it, which reminded me that while I was undergoing a solemn endeavor, I'd best keep my humor intact. And after all, it offers a great opportunity to clean that belly button lint.

Oh, and do you have the linea nigra, the dark track linking navel to belly? It reminded me of the rusty line the dripping faucet left on the back of our porcelain tub. And does your belly have corners? And if you drop a piece of paper, do you try to pick it up with your foot because that's easier than bending over?

I remember in the last few days of my pregnancy taking the car for an oil change. In the waiting room when I entered were a half dozen men, ranging in age from forty to seventy. I was so pregnant that I couldn't wear any shoes besides flip-flops and even my biggest maternity dress was tight across my prodigious pulchritude. I waddled over to a chair and slowly lowered myself, one hand behind me. Suddenly, the baby made such a big flip that I must have inhaled sharply—I could see her ripple across my body in a bumpy wave. At that moment, the door to the garage opened and the worker asked, "Who's next?" And though I was the last one in, all of those men exclaimed, in desperate unison, "She is!"

Not every pregnant woman gets the popped-out belly button and the linea nigra and the belly with corners—friend, I wish them on you.

Love,
Beth Ann

October 21, 2004
Hello, Dear One—

I'm glad—and jealous—Robert's colleagues fed you steak at your baby shower. Almost four years ago, when a group of kind women had a shower for me, they made tea sandwiches so thin you could see through them, little pixie sails to scoot across the bone-china lake of a luncheon plate. They were pretty, these crustless sandwiches, small pastel stripes denoting which was cucumber, which egg salad, which salmon. But my God, at eight months, I didn't want food chosen to match the floral center-piece. I could have stacked a dozen and scarfed them in one bite. I could have snorted them.

I think the hungriest I've ever been in my life was the day after I delivered Claire. Twelve hours of labor and nothing but ice chips, and then waking to the hospital breakfast on its melamine tray: a bran muffin, orange juice, and a banana. Are you kidding me, I asked the attendant, who grinned and rolled her cart away. I wanted T-bones, avocado, beefsteak tomatoes, creamed corn and buttermilk biscuits the way Aunt Tiny makes, cookie dough, andouille, bacon, and sweet potato pie.

After I devoured the breakfast, my friend Monica arrived with cinnamon buns from the bakery and I devoured them, too. Then a colleague's wife arrived, a woman I hardly knew, with a box of Godiva chocolates. I ate the entire first layer, then lifted the black cardboard divider and liberated the bottom layer, too. When the box was empty, the nurses squished down the hall, rolling to my side angry, red, hungry Claire in her clear plastic trolley (looking perhaps like a shrink-wrapped steak herself?). She was screaming in that shaky vibrato newborn way and I held her in that shaky newborn mother way and tried to breast-feed her for the second time ever, watching her furious mouth work to suck to the surface the subterranean stream she could smell but not yet taste because my milk hadn't come in, working and sucking by instinct while my jaw tensed and my womb spasmed as if a taut cord were yanking it toward my nipple and my free hand gripped fistfuls of sheets to anchor me to the bed of pain, and then mysteriously, gradually, the pain lifted and the slits of her eyes closed and a rush of rainbow calm broke upon my naked shoulders and her throat was moving, she was swallowing, and then Claire's mouth slackened off the nipple and she was sleeping, her tongue still flexing, and on her delicious red lower lip stood a single pearl of thin milk. We had done it. I had fed her with my body. I had tasted good to her.

I don't remember Claire being taken out of my arms and put back in the nursery. I do remember kissing the sleeping Claire and then seeing a smudge of Godiva chocolate on her forehead.

So sweet they hurt, these memories. I remember the blue

plastic clamp tying off her stump of umbilical cord. The nurse bringing me clippers to cut Claire's nails, soft and ridged like channeled sand released by low tide. Soon all this will be yours too, then gone, too. You get a one-day-old baby for one day only.

I love that the women who had the shower for you collected advice—it's a great idea. So, to your question. Well, if I'd been at the shower and was asked to contribute my best piece of maternal advice, it would be the advice my old roomie Laura gave me: "The best thing you can do for your child is have a happy marriage."

As much as I loved being with Claire in her infancy, I did at times miss romance, absent from our lives since we were so tired all the time. Even when we were awake and alone together, one of us was sterilizing the pacifiers, another washing the baby's blankets in Dreft. If we rented a movie after Claire was asleep, we couldn't relax into couplehood, as both of us kept an ear cocked for a whimper from the bassinet. Sometimes we'd think we heard her on the monitor and we'd mute the movie, but there would be nothing—we'd begun hearing ghostbabies. And Claire was such a bad sleeper, hardly two hours would pass before we'd hear her milk-thirsty cry, and I'd stumble from bed, as Sylvia Plath writes, "cow-heavy and floral in my Victorian nightgown."

So later, certainly not when she was a newborn but later when she was able to drink from a bottle, we got the chance to go to the beach, and we went. I missed Claire of course, but it was nice to stop missing Tommy, and to stop missing the me I'd been when I was with Tommy. Nice to remember that my breasts had been erogenous zones before they'd been renovated into a twenty-four-hour diner. Nice for Tommy to remember that too. (Oh, no one will tell you this, but sometimes men get jealous of the baby. Tommy didn't, but my neighbor's husband got jealous of their newborn, as did their dog, who started pooping on the floor and chewing through the laundry basket to get at her underwear. Which is mild compared to my friend Patricia's parrot, so aggrieved at the baby in the house that he bloodied his chest beaking out his beautiful citrine feathers. When the baby crawled near the parrot, he'd squawk, "Cover me up! Cover me up!" until they unfurled the gray plastic tarp over his cage.)

Our trip to Italy last summer was the longest we'd been away. I'm sure some mothers raised eyebrows that we'd leave a two-year-old for eight days with her grandparents. Truth is, we both felt guilty on and off, and we missed Claire something awful. But despite what those park-bench judges might insinuate, I don't think she will grow up feeling insecure because her parents abandoned her to go on trips. I hope and think she'll feel secure seeing that her parents still enjoy each other. And that they come home holding sunburned hands with a suitcase of presents for her—and a case of the most lovely Chianti for themselves.

Wish we had some left right now. We could toast to what looks to be your last week of pregnancy. Kathleen, my heart rouses at the thought.

Love,
Beth Ann

P.S. It's cheating, I know, to write this letter on my computer, but because I did I took the opportunity to run spell-check, which didn't have "Godiva" in its dictionary, and suggested "Go, Diva" instead. Pretty fitting, don't you think?

October 25, 2004
Dear One,

I still can't believe it—two days until your due date. I wish I could be shipping myself in this package, but in my place, I hope you'll accept the box of Godiva (Go, Diva).

By the time you get this letter, you'll likely be a mama. You'll hold the whole world in your capable hands.

I've loved sharing this with you. Thank you, sweet friend.

"And now," cried Max, in *Where the Wild Things Are*, "let the wild rumpus start!"

Love, and more love,
Beth Ann

EPILOGUE

On October 28, 2004, Kathleen delivered a healthy ten-pound two-ounce boy she and Robert call Bobby. He's beautiful—I know because the following month when they moved back to Georgia, I made a weekend trip to meet him.

If I were writing fiction, I wouldn't be able to say what happened during my visit. I wouldn't be able to say it because it would smack of coincidence, seem too constructed, too tidy. But in the real world, where truth is stranger than fiction, let me share this strange truth. A rare ice storm hit Georgia and took down power lines, causing an outage. We didn't much care—we'd planned to spend the evening by the fire anyway. So we lit candles and sat around Bobby's blanket and made eyes at him and listened to the storm. When I decided to go to bed, I leaned over to get a candle, and as my arm brushed against my breasts, I realized that they were sore. And that I was pregnant.

Conceived around Labor Day, due on Memorial Day, in my belly the dreamed-of boy child feints and flips. What is he doing—stomping grapes, kneading dough, rubbing kindling to start a fire? Yes, he's starting a fire. Sweet son, we are traveling together toward the burning archway, I'll meet you there. You are the seedling tampened down in the rich dark loam of my body and clamboring toward the light of my second mouth. I'll meet you there. You know me already, I am she fat and happy, she panicked, dated, counting the dates, she blissed and blessed and dreamy, she coursing with Buddha's breath, she obscene lumberer in a stranger's clothes, a stranger's body, she who is a marvel to herself. Oh look at me greening the ripe world, conceive of it, my family of four, of four! And my good husband's goodness at work in your cells, in your bones. Oh what did I do with my hands before they had this round roiling stomach to hold? What did I do with this surfeit of love? I am waiting for you, child. I will take you to my breast.

Thomas Gerald Franklin, III. Or, as Claire misheard it, Thomas Gerbil Franklin.

Scared, yes. Nightmares, yes. Dear-God-I've-been-given-so-much-oh-selfishly-I-beg-one-more-safe-child-one-more-small-flame-to-cup-in-my-hands. And so I step once again onto this shore. Ahead, those circles of women swimming, those voices and those handholds in history, that terrible love and that knowledge. Soon, soon, I will join them: I cannot contain myselves much longer.

Dear K, write me a letter. Send me some advice.

FURTHER INFORMATION ON BOOKS MENTIONED

March 10: *The Pillow Book of Sei Shōnagon*, translated by Ivan Morris. Columbia University Press, 1991.

March 19: *The Mother/Child Papers*, by Alicia Ostriker. Beacon Press, 1986.

April 6: The Anna Akhmatova poem can be found in *Women in Praise of the Sacred: 43 Centuries of Spiritual Poetry by Women*, edited by Jane Hirshfield. HarperPerennial, 1995.

April 8: *The Language Instinct*, by Steven Pinker. William Morrow, 1994.

April 8: I found the essay "Analogy as the Core of Cognition" by Douglas R. Hofstadter in *The Best American Science Writing 2000*, edited by James Gleick and Jesse Cohen. HarperCollins, 2000.

April 26: From *Rough Music*, by Deborah Digges, copyright © 1995 by Deborah Digges. Used by permission of Alfred A. Knopf, a division of Random House, Inc.

April 29: "Metaphors" and "Morning Song" (quoted October 21)

are from *The Collected Poems of Sylvia Plath*. HarperPerennial,
1992.

May 8: *Letters to a Young Poet*, by Rainer Maria Rilke, translated by
M. D. Herter Norton. W. W. Norton, 1993.

June 5: *Journal of a Solitude*, by May Sarton. W. W. Norton, 1993.

June 10: Excerpt from "Bulimia" from *Queen for a Day*, by Denise
Duhamel. © 2001. Reprinted by permission of University of
Pittsburgh Press.

June 16: More Sistine Chapel information from Enrico Bruschini
can be found in his *In the Footsteps of Popes: A Spirited Guide to the
Treasures of the Vatican*. HarperCollins, 2001.

June 22: *The Botany of Desire: A Plant's-Eye View of the World*, by
Michael Pollan. Random House, 2002.

June 22: Margaret Atwood's short story "Giving Birth" was origi-
nally published in *Dancing Girls* (Simon and Schuster, 1977),
but I found it in a wonderful anthology called *Birth: A Literary
Companion*, edited by Kristin Kovacic and Lynne Barrett
(University of Iowa Press, 2002).

June 24: *The House at Pooh Corner*, by A. A. Milne. Dutton Books,
1988.

August 26: Excerpt from "The Language of the Brag" from *Satan
Says*, by Sharon Olds. © 1980. Reprinted by permission of
the University of Pittsburgh Press.

September 17: *Coming of Age with Elephants*, by Joyce Poole.
Hyperion Books, 1997.

September 18: *Dances for Flute and Thunder: Poems from the Ancient*

Greek, translated by Brooks Haxton. Viking Penguin, 1999.

September 22: *The Glass Anvil,* by Andrew Hudgins. University of Michigan Press, 1997.

September 25: "Ars Poetica?" is from *The Collected Poems* by Czeslaw Milosz (Ecco Press, 1988).

October 8: *Intimate Adversaries: Cultural Conflicts Between Doctors and Women Patients,* by Alexandra Dundas Todd. University of Pennsylvania Press, 1989.

October 25: *Where the Wild Things Are,* by Maurice Sendak. HarperCollins, 1963.

ACKNOWLEDGMENTS

This book is a tribute to friendship, particularly the friendship between women that sustains and guides and comforts. I'd like to thank the many friends who have sustained and guided and comforted me: first, thanks to Kathleen, who encouraged me to write these letters, and then encouraged me to share them. I'd like to thank my oldest friends, my mother, Mary Anna Malich, and my sister, Julie Fennelly. Thanks to Gerald and Betty Franklin, loving folks who raised a loving son. Thanks to Jane Paglini and Patricia Lippens. Continued thanks to my college roommates, Laura Hajdukiewicz, Denise Karkos, Beth Louder, and Carmen Nanni. Thanks as well to my Oxford friends, Dorothy Howorth, Mary Hartwell Howorth, Vivian Neill, Linda Peal, and Lisa Williams, and especially Blair Hobbs and Ann Fisher-Wirth, kind poet pals who read these letters prior to publication. Thanks to Kathy Poires for her vision and generosity. To Judith Weber: it's my good fortune to have you on my side. To the incomparable Carol Houck Smith: you are the good witch who provides the ruby slippers and points out the yellow brick road. To my best friend, and my more-than-friend, Tommy: you give me the confidence to try to be the person you believe I am. Because of you: everything. To Claire, and to her expected baby brother, Thomas: thank you, and when you're sulky teenagers, forgive me for writing about you, my sweet inspirations.